Ellen

DeGeneres

Groundbreaking Television Star

W9-CHM-465

By Jennifer Lombardo

Portions of this book originally appeared in
Ellen DeGeneres by Katie Sharp.

LUCENT
PRESS

Published in 2019 by
Lucent Press, an Imprint of Greenhaven Publishing, LLC
353 3rd Avenue
Suite 255
New York, NY 10010

Designer: Deanna Paternostro
Editor: Jennifer Lombardo

Cataloging-in-Publication Data

Names: Lombardo, Jennifer.
Title: Ellen DeGeneres: groundbreaking television star / Jennifer Lombardo.
Description: New York : Lucent Press, 2019. | Series: People in the news |
Includes index.
Identifiers: ISBN 9781534563346 (pbk.) | ISBN 9781534563322 (library bound) |
ISBN 9781534563339 (ebook)
Subjects: LCSH: DeGeneres, Ellen–Juvenile literature. | Comedians–United
States–Biography–Juvenile literature. | Television personalities–United States–
Biography–Juvenile literature.
Classification: LCC PN228.D358 L66 2019 | DDC 792.702'8092 B–dc23

Printed in the United States of America

CPSIA compliance information: Batch #BS18KL: For further information contact Greenhaven Publishing LLC, New York,
New York at 1-844-317-7404.

Please visit our website, www.greenhavenpublishing.com. For a free color
catalog of all our high-quality books, call toll free 1-844-317-7404 or fax
1-844-317-7405.

Contents

Foreword   4

Introduction   6
   Never Giving Up

Chapter One   10
   Early Life

Chapter Two   25
   Getting Her Start

Chapter Three   37
   A Brave Woman

Chapter Four   55
   A Groundbreaking Episode

Chapter Five   70
   The Star of the Show

Notes   90

Ellen DeGeneres Year by Year   96

For More Information   98

Index   100

Picture Credits   103

About the Author   104

Foreword

We live in a world where the latest news is always available and where it seems we have unlimited access to the lives of the people in the news. Entire television networks are devoted to news about politics, sports, and entertainment. Social media has allowed people to have an unprecedented level of interaction with celebrities. We have more information at our fingertips than ever before. However, how much do we really know about the people we see on television news programs, social media feeds, and magazine covers?

Despite the constant stream of news, the full stories behind the lives of some of the world's most newsworthy men and women are often unknown. Who was Katy Perry before she was a pop music phenomenon? What does LeBron James do when he's not playing basketball? What inspires Lin-Manuel Miranda?

This series aims to answer questions like these about some of the biggest names in pop culture, sports, politics, and technology. While the subjects of this series come from all walks of life and areas of expertise, they share a common magnetism that has made them all captivating figures in the public eye. They have shaped the world in some unique way, and—in many cases—they are poised to continue to shape the world for many years to come.

These biographies are not just a collection of basic facts. They tell compelling stories that show how each figure grew to become a powerful public personality. Each book aims to paint a complete, realistic picture of its subject—from the challenges they overcame to the controversies they caused. In doing so, each book reinforces the idea that even the most famous faces on the news are real people who are much more complex than we are often shown in brief video clips or sound bites. Readers are also reminded that there is even more to a person than what they present to the world through social media posts, press releases, and interviews. The whole story of a person's life can only be discovered by digging beneath the surface of their public persona, and that is what this series allows readers to do.

The books in this series are filled with enlightening quotes from speeches and interviews given by the subjects, as well as quotes and anecdotes from those who know their story best: family, friends, coaches, and colleagues. All quotes are noted to provide guidance for further research. Detailed lists of additional resources are also included, as are timelines, indexes, and unique photographs. These text features come together to enhance the reading experience and encourage readers to dive deeper into the stories of these influential men and women.

Fame can be fleeting, but the subjects featured in this series have real staying power. They have fundamentally impacted their respective fields and have achieved great success through hard work and true talent. They are men and women defined by their accomplishments, and they are often seen as role models for the next generation. They have left their mark on the world in a major way, and their stories are meant to inspire readers to leave their mark, too.

Introduction

Never
Giving Up

Ellen DeGeneres is a well-known celebrity. Her daytime talk show, *The Ellen DeGeneres Show*, averages about 2.9 million viewers per episode, according to a 2010 report, and the week of December 9, 2013, she averaged 4.4 million—the highest in the show's history at that point, according to *Variety* magazine. However, in 2014, after she hosted the Oscars, her show broke that record with an audience of 4.8 million.

Even people who do not watch her show know who DeGeneres is. She has used her signature brand of comedy to host award shows such as the Oscars and Emmy Awards as well as the highly rated sketch show *Saturday Night Live*. She has also won multiple awards not only for her comedy but also for her charity work, and she has been an outspoken champion of social justice in everyday life.

About 20 years ago, such success seemed impossible for this stand-up comedian from New Orleans, Louisiana. At what seemed to be the height of her career, in 1997—with a successful stand-up career, a hit television sitcom, and a best-selling book—DeGeneres decided to announce publicly that she is a lesbian. Although many had already assumed that she was, she wanted to set the record straight, to address the rumors and gossip. DeGeneres timed her announcement so that she and her character, Ellen Morgan, whom she played on her television show *Ellen*, would come out at about the same time. What DeGeneres wanted to do would make television history: Ellen Morgan would be the first lesbian lead in a television sitcom.

Although many colleagues and friends questioned DeGeneres's decision, the comedian knew exactly what she was doing. She wanted to be true to herself. She did not want to hide who she was anymore. Many people, including those who identify as lesbian, gay, bisexual, transgender, or other nontraditional sexualities and gender identities (LGBT+), applauded her move; others, including some high-profile religious leaders and the show's sponsors, were not happy and disapproved of her decision. Many others were somewhere in the middle; they did not care that DeGeneres was a lesbian, they simply did not think it was necessary for her to be so open about her sexuality. They wanted to laugh at her comedy without knowing the details of her life.

Many people have seen at least one episode of *The Ellen DeGeneres Show,* and most major celebrities have been on it.

As one of the first female celebrities to openly talk about the fact that she is a lesbian, DeGeneres has helped pave the way for other members of the LGBT+ community. At a time when discrimination against LGBT+ people was even more widespread than it is today and few people were openly "out," DeGeneres's action showed incredible courage and made her a role model for many.

Although the episode in which Ellen's character revealed her sexuality was well received by both fans and critics and DeGeneres was nominated for two Emmy Awards for it, her show was canceled in 1998. DeGeneres felt that her fans and the entertainment industry had turned on her. She was certain nobody liked her anymore. She began to get fewer offers for work. However, instead of hiding out and feeling sorry for herself, she again showed courage and went back to the career she had started out in: stand-up comedy.

A Natural Comedian

As a child, DeGeneres did not aspire to make people laugh—she just did it naturally. With her family making constant moves around the New Orleans area, DeGeneres found herself having to start over in a new school and make new friends time after time. She used her gift of humor to make the people around her notice her; she made friends by making people laugh.

So when the time came for DeGeneres to pick herself up and get her career on the right track again, she wrote a comedy routine appropriately called *The Beginning* and took it on the road. She filmed the show for HBO, and audiences loved it. However, what really turned her career around was her ability to make Americans laugh again following the September 11, 2001, terrorist attacks on New York City's World Trade Center towers and the Pentagon in Washington, D.C. Hosting the Emmy Awards just two months after the tragedy, she received rave reviews and a standing ovation for her delicate handling of the show. Since that time, DeGeneres has found herself working steadily as her career rebounded.

Ellen DeGeneres grew up in New Orleans, shown here.

Soon after hosting the 2001 Emmy Awards show, DeGeneres found herself much in demand. She voiced Dory the fish in the films *Finding Nemo* and *Finding Dory*, did another HBO comedy special, and started what would become her award-winning talk show. She also has helped the citizens of her native New Orleans in the aftermath of Hurricane Katrina; started a pet food company; married the love of her life, Portia de Rossi; became a spokesmodel for CoverGirl; and achieved much more in both her public and private life.

With all the ups and downs in her life, Ellen DeGeneres has shown everyone around her what it takes to persevere in show business and in life—laughter.

Chapter **One**

Early Life

Ellen DeGeneres had a relatively unusual upbringing; her family moved often, and she was raised a Christian Scientist—a religious sect that believes in using prayer to heal ailments rather than modern medicine. However, despite these things that set her apart from her peers, DeGeneres seemed like an average child, according to those who knew her when she was young. Although she had a cheerful personality and a good sense of humor, there was no indication, early on, that she would grow up to be one of the most famous comedians of the 21st century.

The DeGeneres Family

Ellen DeGeneres described the beginning of her life in her 1995 best-selling book, *My Point … and I Do Have One*: "I was born in Jefferson Parish, Louisiana, at Ochsner Hospital, January 26, 1958. I lived in a house on Haring Road in Metairie until I was … oh, let's say eight or nine—maybe ten … could've been seven or six, I don't know."[1]

Metairie, which is located in Jefferson Parish, is a suburb of New Orleans. DeGeneres's parents, Elliott and Elizabeth— who often goes by the nickname Betty—already had a four-year-old son, Vance, when Ellen was born. In her 1999 book,

Ellen DeGeneres has written about important parts of her life, including her childhood.

Love, Ellen: A Mother/Daughter Journey, Betty DeGeneres wrote of having to convince her husband to have another child: "Ellen was indeed a miracle. I had to beg for a second child. Elliott thought one child, whom we dearly loved, was sufficient. Nothing if not tenacious, I didn't give up. I thank God every day that I persevered, and so does Elliott."[2]

Elliott was an insurance salesman; Betty worked as an administrative assistant while also taking care of their two children. Both were devoted Christian Scientists, which is how they met, and they raised their children in the faith as well. According to Betty, the family relied on prayer as its guide, and as Christian Scientists, her children never received vaccinations or medications of any kind and attended Sunday school to learn about the Bible and prayer. Betty believed giving her children a strong spiritual foundation was a good, important thing—that all children need to know that, like their parents, God loves them just the way they are, no matter what.

In *My Point ... and I Do Have One*, Ellen talked about growing up a Christian Scientist:

> I was raised a Christian Scientist and was taught to believe that we could heal our bodies through prayer, that sickness was an illusion that could be defeated by the power of the spirit ... I didn't take my first aspirin until I was in my teens and even now I feel a twinge of guilt when I go to the pharmacy.[3]

In addition to spiritual healing, Ellen said, the religion placed emphasis on hiding emotion and pretending things were fine when they were not. In a 2016 interview with *Parade* magazine, she said,

> I didn't see deep emotion from my parents. It was all very polite and very surface. I never knew how anybody was feeling. Because of that religion everything was fine all the time ...
>
> That's not a healthy way to grow up. It was very hard to express yourself. A kid should be told that you can have feelings. I have a

lot of feelings. You can feel sad and angry and hurt. But the only feeling that was approved of is happiness—that was it. How can you have happiness when you're not honest?[4]

Controversy Over Christian Science

Christian Science is a religious movement founded in 1879 by Mary Baker Eddy. Although the church declares that all medical decisions are based on individual choice, Christian Scientists generally do not seek traditional medical care for illnesses, instead relying on their faith and spirituality to heal. While some support this as a choice of religious freedom, others believe it puts people in danger, especially children. In some cases, parents have been charged with child abuse or neglect when their decision not to treat their child's illness resulted in death. In 2015, Washington State passed a bill stating that people would no longer be able to cite religious beliefs as a reason not to get their child vaccinated or seek medical care for them.

As she grew up, there were no obvious signs that Ellen would one day become a successful comedian. Classmates recalled her being no different than anyone else; she never tried to be the class clown or the center of attention. She enjoyed riding her bike around the city and had a great love of animals. She told an interviewer, "I was obsessed with animals, and I really thought I'd join the Peace Corps or go to Africa and study apes or be a veterinarian."[5] However, she was also fascinated with performers on TV—especially comedians.

When Ellen was in third grade, her family made its first move. Elliott would move the family quite a bit over the next several

As a child, DeGeneres thought about becoming
a veterinarian, and she still loves animals.

years. The constant changes took their toll on Ellen and made it hard for her to feel like she fit in. Adding to that feeling was the fact that she was a Christian Scientist. She has memories of other students lining up for vaccinations, but she was the only one who did not have to because of her religion. Even though she was afraid of needles and thus did not want to get a shot, she recalled crying because she wanted to be in the line with everyone else.

Dealing with Change

With all the moves and struggles to fit in, the early 1970s brought more change and difficulties for Ellen. In 1970, after Betty's father died of a heart attack, Betty decided she no longer wanted to be a practicing Christian Scientist. She felt strongly that if her father had been given better health care, he may have survived his heart attack. She also found that the religion offered her no comfort as she grieved for her father. For a few more years, however, Ellen and Vance continued to be practicing Christian Scientists, going to church with their father.

Once Betty made the decision to leave the Christian Scientist faith, she and Elliott lost one of the strongest bonds that had held them together. So, in 1971, she made another decision that would greatly affect Ellen: Betty planned to leave Elliott. For years, she had not been happy in her marriage, and now she felt it had reached the breaking point. Walking with young Ellen one day, Betty spotted a "for rent" sign outside an apartment complex. She shared her plan with her daughter. In *Love, Ellen*, Betty talked about that moment:

> *El [Ellen] was the one who saw through it. I think she knew before I did that her parents' marriage was ending … Young as she was, she was well aware of my feeling of desperation. "This will be fun," El said in an instinctive effort to cheer me up, and then went on to describe all the adventures Vance, she, and I would have as a bachelor and bachelorettes. Not to mention that it would be a nice change for her pet snake.*[6]

Ever since DeGeneres was young, she and her mother have been close.

Supporting Betty through the divorce was just the first of many occasions in which Ellen would use her good nature, wit, and humor to help cheer up her mother, which planted the seed that would eventually bloom into a career as a stand-up comic. Ellen reflected on that time in an interview:

My mother was going through a hard time. She dated lots of really horrible men and had bad experiences ... I had to make her laugh. [My comedy] started from me trying to make her happy. It felt really good to have power to make people happy. That's my talent. Not that I thought I'd make money from it.[7]

On Their Own

After Betty and Elliott separated, Betty and Ellen moved into a small apartment in Lake Vista, another area of New Orleans, and Elliott got an apartment nearby. Vance was in a touring band at the time, and his travels left Ellen and Betty alone together—a lot. While the two were already very close, their bond grew even deeper. They talked about the boys Ellen had her eye on—often out-of-reach rock stars. They went clothes shopping and ate out. As they shared their favorite cheesecake, Ellen would entertain her mother with quirky observations about everyday life and situations. Ellen was also very thoughtful to her mother, making sure her coworkers recognized her on her birthday and giving her personalized gifts.

With their last move, Ellen did not have to switch high schools again. Even so, she still had trouble fitting in among her peers. Her Christian Scientist faith continued to make her feel like an outsider. In *My Point ... and I Do Have One*, she wrote,

> *Because I was raised Christian Scientist, I was excused from all my high school science classes; I wasn't supposed to learn about the human body. On the plus side, I never had to dissect a frog ... The negative side ... was that for the longest time I didn't know anything about the human body at all. When my stomach hurt, I said I had a stomachcake—I didn't know it was a stomachache. While that sort of mistake is cute in a four-year-old, in a teenager it raises a few eyebrows.*[8]

Later, Ellen would speak about those less-than-happy high school days: "Back then in New Orleans I didn't have any hangouts; I moved around too much for that. I had a lot of different friends, but all the time I was trying to find myself. I didn't know who I really wanted to be—or what I wanted to be."[9]

Ellen decided to assert herself as an individual in an attempt to find out just who she was. Her first step was to stop being a Christian Scientist. She also started hanging out with an older, questionable crowd. She and her mother were living in an area of Metairie that had a lot of nightclubs. Ellen and some friends she had met at high school were somehow getting into one of the nightclubs, even though they were too young. Ellen also told Betty that one of her friends who was working at the mall was stealing jewelry. All of this worried Betty. She did not want to see her daughter go down the wrong path.

Betty's Remarriage

Although Betty left Elliott in 1971, their divorce was not final until 1973. At that point, she was ready to be in a relationship again. The apartment complex where they lived had a pool, which is where Betty met a man with whom she became serious and eventually married. In her book, *Love, Ellen*, Betty referred to this man only by the initial B, because of events that would later take place.

B was divorced and had three children. Betty thought he was a strong father figure and might offer Ellen some discipline, which Betty felt her daughter needed. He was a salesman and had sold Betty on his good looks, take-charge attitude, and know-how about cars, gardening, and home repair.

Soon after Betty married B, they decided to move to the small town of Atlanta, Texas, with a population of just around 6,000. Betty thought the move would be good for them. Although Ellen eventually moved with them, Vance decided to stay in New Orleans and live with Elliott. Not wanting to take Ellen out of school in the middle of the year, they decided she would join them in June. In the meantime, Ellen would also live with her father. Ellen was not happy about the move. She knew what it meant: She would have to start all over yet again.

When June arrived, Ellen moved to Texas and had to adjust to the slower pace of life in a small town. According to Betty, Ellen quickly made friends and joined the high school tennis team, but she did not participate in many of the activities other teenagers were doing at the time. In an interview in 1993, Ellen reflected on the move and life in small-town Texas:

> I was hanging out with people who were older, staying out late, and I think that was one of the reasons my mother thought it would be good to move to Atlanta, Texas … We lived in a dry county, which meant that teenagers would drive 45 miles for beer … At that time, the height of aspirations was to get your name in iridescent letters on the back of your boyfriend's pickup truck. You can see why the day after graduation from high school, I headed back to New Orleans.[10]

However, Ellen again used her humor to fit in and make new friends in Texas. Later she would say, "Instead of being the pretty girl people flocked to, I was the one who said something to make them pay attention."[11] However, it was still not easy for her to fit in. For one thing, she was sensitive about the fact that she had gained some weight before her move to Texas, consoling herself with food since learning about having to move. Additionally,

DeGeneres has always preferred big cities such as New Orleans, shown here, to small towns such as Atlanta, Texas.

Vance DeGeneres

Ellen's brother, Vance DeGeneres, tried comedy before Ellen did. In fact, Ellen was often referred to as "Vance's sister" because he was better known than she was. In 1977, he and two friends came up with an idea for a short movie about a simple clay figure named Mr. Bill who always had very bad luck—he often ended up flattened like a pancake. They filmed the movie, *Home Movie: The Mr. Bill Show*, and submitted it to *Saturday Night Live*, which quickly accepted it. Vance had a part in the movie; he was Mr. Hands, the archenemy of Mr. Bill. After the first episode of the *Mr. Bill Show* aired, audiences loved it, so more episodes were ordered.

Unfortunately, Vance had some bad luck of his own and had a falling out with his partners. They went to court, with Vance trying to get a portion of the rights to Mr. Bill along with some of the profits. They settled out of court for an undisclosed amount.

Vance then made music his career. He had played in bands since junior high school, and in the early 1980s,

she was feeling homesick for New Orleans and suffered bouts of depression. However, she put on a good face, doing her best to smile and be cheerful. Classmates and teachers from her high school remembered her as being a good student with a good sense of humor.

Ellen also went on dates with boys and even had steady boyfriends throughout high school. During her senior year, she became serious with a boy named Ben. He gave her a promise ring (a ring that is a symbol of commitment between two people), and for a while, she was convinced she wanted to marry him. However, the relationship ended when Ben went to college and Ellen ended up moving back to New Orleans. In a 2014 interview, Ben said he felt they would have remained friends he played the bass and wrote songs for the punk rock band the Cold. In the mid-1980s, Vance cofounded a band called House of Schock, but it did not last very long. In 1998, he joined the band Cowboy Mouth and stayed with it until 2007, when he left to pursue television projects. Today, Vance lives near his sister and mother in California and co-runs Carousel Productions, actor and comedian Steve Carrell's production company.

Ellen's brother, Vance, also works in television.

if they had been able to live in the same place. It was around this time that Ellen started to feel she was actually attracted to women; she later mentioned that she and her best female friend had been physically intimate while she was dating Ben, but said that at the time, because no one talked openly about homosexuality, she thought her relationships were typical—that this was just how best friends acted. She realized this was not true when she met another girl she was attracted to. However, these feelings confused her, and she tried to ignore them as a teenager.

A Difficult Time

In 1975, after Betty discovered a lump in her right breast, she made an appointment for a medical procedure called a biopsy to have it studied. Ellen wanted to go to the hospital with her mother that day, but Betty convinced her it was not necessary.

While performing the biopsy, the doctors found that the lump was malignant, or cancerous, so they removed her entire breast—without Betty's knowledge. While she was under anesthesia, B had given the doctors permission to do the procedure. For the next two days in the hospital, Ellen was constantly at her mother's side. As Betty recalled,

> B was in and out, but El hardly left my side. We had seen each other through a lot of loss already. But this was different. We had no experience whatsoever with illness ... To see me lying in that bed, dejected and shocked, must have been terrifying for Ellen. And yet she remained strong and calm, attending to my every need.[12]

In an interview with *USA Today* in 2007, Betty and Ellen talked about helping each other through this hard time: "Everything was a little dirty secret back then," Ellen said. "The fact that she [Betty] had a mastectomy was not spoken of. She tried to shield me from it a little bit, but she needed my help with recovery and physical rehabilitation. It bonded us even more." Betty agreed, "It's a very special relationship that I do not take for granted. We've been there for each other."[13]

With high school graduation fast approaching, Ellen had no idea what she wanted to do next. She really did not like school and had no desire to go to college. She enjoyed playing tennis but was not good enough to play professionally. She also played golf and sang, but she doubted she could make a career of either one. She also knew she did not want to work as a secretary or in a factory. B was not happy with Ellen's lack of goals and motivation; Betty described him as "bossy ... harsh and mean-spirited,"[14] someone who wanted things done his way. For instance, he once

In 1975, Betty DeGeneres underwent a mastectomy, which is a medical procedure in which one breast is removed. Ellen and her mother have been open about this difficult time.

yelled at Ellen for the way she was cleaning the toilet. She started to cry, and Betty came to her rescue. Betty recalled, "I could see the conflict in her face. On the one hand, she was furious with the man I had chosen to be my husband; on the other hand, she loved me and wanted me to be happy with him."[15] During this time, Ellen often stayed away from home just to avoid B.

Although Ellen DeGeneres was not sure what she wanted to do with her life, one thing was certain: She did not want to stay in Atlanta. Small-town life was not for her, so she made plans to move back to Louisiana and live with her father and his new wife until she could afford a place of her own. She would leave the day after graduation. Betty was heartsick, but she knew she could not stop her daughter. In June 1976, when moving day arrived, DeGeneres packed up her yellow Volkswagen and hugged her mother goodbye.

Chapter Two

Getting Her Start

As she got older, Ellen DeGeneres knew she wanted to do something with her life, but she was still not sure what. She tried getting a college degree and working in several different fields, but nothing clicked; she knew she would not be happy with any of them in the long term. At the same time, she was coming to terms with her own sexuality. In general, as it is for most people, DeGeneres's early adulthood was a time of soul-searching, experimentation, and self-discovery—all of which would eventually pay off.

Back in New Orleans

Happy to be back in New Orleans, but with no job, DeGeneres decided to give college a try. She enrolled as a communications student at the University of New Orleans. Although she hated school, she went to college because it is what everyone else her age was doing. However, she remembered sitting in lectures and thinking that whatever the subject matter was—the history of Greek theater, for example—it was not what she wanted to know about.

DeGeneres was a college student for just one semester. She then spent her time looking for work—and she found it, again and again. She held some jobs for weeks or months; others lasted only a few hours. How long she lasted depended on how bored or restless she became. She held a variety of jobs: She was an employment counselor, babysat children, worked at a car wash, wrapped packages in a department store, did accounting for a wig store, worked at a chain clothing store, shucked oysters, worked as a landscaper, painted houses, waited tables, and even sold vacuum cleaners.

It was during this time in her life that she came to terms with the fact that she was a lesbian. Because she was in New Orleans—a big, liberal city—she was able to find a group of people among whom she felt comfortable, who allowed her to be herself. She went to gay bars, started to date women, and

Taking Comedy from Real Life

DeGeneres's time as a vacuum cleaner salesperson was the inspiration for one of the first jokes she used in her stand-up routine. She would say, "I'd go to different stores and demonstrate when people were shopping. I'd throw mud in front of them. That's what I did. Boy, did that job suck."[1]

DeGeneres also found humor to be a useful selling tool. She said she was good at coming up with something funny to help connect with people and make a sale. She told a story in which the most expensive vacuum cleaner had a light on the front of it. She was trying to sell one to a woman who asked her why she would need a light on the front of her vacuum cleaner. DeGeneres joked, "That's so you can vacuum at night and not wake people up by turning on the lights."[2] The woman bought the vacuum cleaner.

even fell in love with a woman named Kat.

Although DeGeneres had friends and felt at home in New Orleans, she struggled with what to do with herself. She realized she had been in New Orleans for three years and had yet to find a calling that she felt passionate about—something she wanted to do the rest of her life. She also realized that something important was missing in her life: her mother. DeGeneres tried three times to move back to Atlanta, but it never worked out; she wanted to be with her mother, but she hated the town too much to stay.

Betty was always happy to see Ellen. Being apart was hard on both of them. Ellen needed time to figure out what she was going to do with her life, and Betty was more than happy to give her that time. However, B was not happy with the

As a reference to her old stand-up routine, DeGeneres used a vacuum cleaner while hosting the Oscars.

1. Quoted in Kathleen Tracy, *Ellen: The Real Story of Ellen DeGeneres*. Secaucus, NJ: Carol, 1999, p. 46.

2. Quoted in Tracy, *Ellen*, p. 46.

situation. He could not understand why Betty was so patient with her daughter; he felt Ellen should have been working. During this time, Ellen started to do some writing. She wrote humor pieces that she thought she might submit to magazines such as *Ms.* and *National Lampoon*. She never did submit them, however. Instead, she stored them away while she struggled to find her calling.

Coming Out

Back in New Orleans, DeGeneres eventually moved in with Kat. According to those around them, the two were friends and then fell deeply in love. Kat was a poet, and DeGeneres thought the two would be together forever. Encouraged by her girlfriend, DeGeneres continued to write. She never sent anything out to magazines, but she shared her work with Kat and Betty.

A few months after DeGeneres made her last move back to New Orleans, she decided it was time to be honest about her sexuality with the person who meant the most to her— her mother. In 1978, while 20-year-old DeGeneres and her mother were on a trip to Pass Christian, Mississippi, to visit Betty's sister and her family, Ellen and Betty took a stroll along the beach.

Ellen confessed to Betty that she had fallen in love. Betty was thrilled for her daughter and told her so. However, then, Ellen revealed the whole truth: She was in love with a woman. In *Love, Ellen*, Betty recalled,

As she cried and I hugged her, a hailstorm of conflicting emotions continued to pummel me from every direction. There was my shock and disbelief, yes, together with my fear … As it must be for all mothers, the prospect of either one of my kids being hurt was unbearable. And with this revelation from Ellen, I was probably even more scared, mainly because of my ignorance. How could I protect her from the unknown?

When she was 20 years old, DeGeneres told her mother the truth about her sexuality.

> *Since I couldn't, my irrational impulse was somehow to convince her that this wasn't really who she was. And so, when I asked, "Maybe this is just a phase?" Ellen took it to mean that I was ashamed of her.*[16]

Being openly gay was not as common in the 20th century as it is in the 21st, and it was something that was not well understood. The term LGBT+ had not yet been created to describe all the various members of the community, so most people were only aware of gay men and women—and many believed negative myths about them. However, some people were able to understand that the personality of their loved one did not change when they declared their sexuality.

Today, there are LGBT+ pride parades held around the world, but these did not start until 1970. In the recent past, fewer people admitted to being anything but heterosexual.

Although Betty was shocked, she always knew she would love her daughter no matter what. After all, this is what she had taught both of her children. She was not ashamed of Ellen, but she admitted she knew nothing about homosexuality, and she wanted to understand her daughter and what she would be going through. So Betty quickly learned what she could about homosexuality, reading books and articles about the topic. In a 2004 interview with Stone Phillips on *Dateline NBC*, DeGeneres talked about telling her mother the truth:

> *First of all, she didn't understand it, and then she went to the library and read about homosexuality, which I can only*

imagine what those books were. You know? She probably first got Homo sapiens [the scientific term for human] and read that. That's probably the only book they had. Well, what's wrong with that? So what, she's a Homo sapiens? Aren't we all? But, see, she was great. All this—thought it was a phase. And she thought I'd, you know, go through it and—like the tube top. Oh, she won't wear that after a certain amount of time.[17]

As Betty struggled to understand what her daughter was going through, she had many questions, including whether Ellen would have children. She discussed her concerns with Ellen, and at one point asked her if maybe she just had not yet met the right young man.

Later that year, when Ellen brought a man home to celebrate Christmas, Betty thought maybe Ellen might not be gay after all. However, after seeing her and the man together, Betty knew "the right man wasn't going to 'save' Ellen. She didn't need saving. What a breakthrough that realization was for me!"[18] Soon, Ellen felt more comfortable bringing Betty into her circle of friends. Betty wrote, "El had once said that I probably would never completely understand. I'm happy to say she was wrong about that. I'm even happier that she was willing to give me time—to learn, to reason, to see. That's all I needed."[19]

Betty would eventually do much more than completely understand—she would become her daughter's greatest supporter and an advocate for the LGBT+ community, helping other families learn to accept their children for who they truly are.

Ellen's father, Elliott, on the other hand, did not take the news as well. At the time she told him she was gay, Ellen was living with him; his wife, Virginia; and Virginia's two daughters. When Ellen told them about her sexuality, Elliott and Virginia asked her to move out. They told her they thought she would be a bad influence on her young stepsisters.

Elliott was not going to let Ellen be homeless, however.

Encouraging Others

A good way to sum up just who Ellen DeGeneres is and why she is such a symbol of perseverance is to read the commencement speech she gave to the class of 2009 at Tulane University in New Orleans. In speaking about what happened after she came out in 1997, she said,

> The phone didn't ring for three years. I had no offers. Nobody wanted to touch me at all. Yet, I was getting letters from kids that almost committed suicide, but didn't, because of what I did. And I realized that I had a purpose ... Really when I look back on it, I wouldn't change a thing. I mean, it was so important for me to lose everything because I found out what the most important thing is, is to be true to yourself. Ultimately, that's what's gotten me to this place. I don't live in fear, I'm free, I have no secrets. And I know I'll always be OK, because no matter what, I know who I am.
>
> And as you grow, you'll realize the definition of success changes ... For me, the most important thing in your life is to live your life with integrity—and not to give into peer pressure, to try to be something that you're not—to live your life as an honest and compassionate person, to contribute in some way ... Follow your passion, stay true to yourself. Never follow anyone else's path, unless you're in the woods and you're lost and you see a path, and by all means you should follow that. Don't give advice, it will come back and bite you ... Don't take anyone's advice. So my advice to you is to be true to yourself and everything will be fine.[1]

---

1. Ellen DeGeneres, "In Case You Missed My Tulane Speech, Watch It Here," *The Ellen DeGeneres Show*, June 26, 2009. ellen.warnerbros.com/2009/06/in_case_you_missed_my_tulane_s.php.

He helped her get a loan so she could pay for an apartment. DeGeneres was hurt by her father's reaction, but she still loved him. Later, she told an interviewer, "I didn't acknowledge it for years, that was bad, because they loved me and I loved them, and yet they didn't want me in the house. They didn't want that to be around her little girls."[20]

Later, Elliott admitted that it was not right for him to tell Ellen to leave. "I was wrong, just that simple. Was it ignorance? I don't know. I never really studied it or read about it and thought about it. I guess when you don't have all the facts in anything, that's a factor of some ignorance."[21] When he died in January 2018 at the age of 92, DeGeneres described him on her show as a loving, nonjudgmental man who made it clear that he was proud of her and what she had accomplished. She also noted that her sense of humor was strongly influenced by his.

Keeping It Secret

Although DeGeneres was honest with those closest to her, she did not come out to everyone. She kept her sexuality a secret from the public for almost 20 more years. Many people had their suspicions, but DeGeneres and her mother did their best to put off the questions and comments. This secret they carried between them strengthened their bond even more.

In 1980, DeGeneres was selling season subscriptions to plays at Saenger Theatre in New Orleans. Soon, she was hanging out with theater people, which gave her the idea of doing stand-up comedy. Sometime between August 4 and September 9 of that year, DeGeneres performed her first routine. Some friends asked DeGeneres to help them out with a luncheon benefit. DeGeneres recalled,

> Somebody needed to raise money for something, and no one had access to Eddie Murphy or Aerosmith, so they put a band together and asked me to go onstage and be funny … I had no material; I had nothing to talk about. I couldn't think of

anything funny. So I ate the whole time I was up there.

I always thought it was funny when people have something to tell you and they take a huge bite of something, and then they make you wait, to finish that bite. And then when they're halfway through the sentence, they take another bite.

So I got onstage and said, "I gotta tell you about the funniest thing that happened to me the other day. But I'm sorry, this is the only chance I'm going to get to sit down and eat today, so if you don't mind, I'm going to eat my lunch."[22]

DeGeneres started to tell her "story" and took a bite of a hamburger she had bought on her way to the show. Her audience, though small, loved the routine and they loved DeGeneres. Later, when she talked about that experience, she would say she loved it and that it gave her the greatest feeling. Right after the show, someone approached DeGeneres about appearing at a coffeehouse on the campus of the University of New Orleans. She agreed right away but then felt nervous, worried she would not have enough material. That night, she looked over the material she had written years earlier for magazines but had never submitted. Suddenly, she was filled with confidence. What she had written would be perfect for a stand-up routine. She added a few more stories, and she was ready.

DeGeneres received good reviews—as well as $15 and a mention in the *Times Picayune* newspaper—for her coffeehouse show. She clipped the article and sent it to her mother, who was still in Texas. DeGeneres was soon asked to perform at other small venues at other colleges in the area. Betty drove to New Orleans and invited a cousin to go see DeGeneres perform. Elliott was also there that night. At first, Betty admitted, she thought stand-up comedy was going to be just another one of her daughter's passing interests. However, after just 10 minutes of watching her daughter perform, Betty felt this was definitely different:

Working in a theater was what started DeGeneres on the road to stand-up comedy.

Since I've never been a fan of jokes, I was pleased to see that Ellen didn't tell jokes; instead she told funny stories and played off real or imagined situations. Her delivery, even then, was crisp—with her deadpan, fresh-faced, girl next-door expression, she made the absurd even more laughable … After the performance, Ellen came out and sat with us, accepting a round of congratulations and praise. After all the others had their say, it was my turn. First, I gave her a big hug and told her how great she was. And then I added, "El, I'll help you in any way I can." I knew this was it. She was really on to something.[23]

A Sense of Purpose

Finally feeling as though she had found her calling, DeGeneres took her mother up on her offer to help. In October 1980, she wrote to Betty and asked if she would buy her a cassette player. She wanted to record her routines and study them so she could perfect her delivery. In return, DeGeneres said, she would one day repay her with a brand-new car or a condominium in Dallas, Texas. Betty was more than happy to help, and DeGeneres worked on her comedy with renewed enthusiasm.

By November, however, her energy started to wane. Comedy work did not come, and she was running out of money. In December, her luck changed when she landed her first real comedy gig. DeGeneres felt good about her future. She got busy polishing her material and writing new routines. She had come a long way, from doing odd jobs to finally feeling like she had found her true calling. Over the next several years, she worked hard to make a name for herself—fueled by both comedy and tragedy.

Chapter **Three**

A Brave Woman

Ellen DeGeneres has faced many difficult situations throughout her life. In addition to coming out at a time when being gay was something most people did not want to hear about, she has dealt with the death of her first love, the struggle to make a career out of her passion, and the pressures of celebrity life. However, through it all, she has kept moving forward, holding onto her cheerful outlook and encouraging others with her positivity and bravery.

Turning Tragedy into Experience

As the 1980s began, DeGeneres started getting more and more excited about the prospect of a career in comedy. However, just as her life was looking up, she experienced a great personal tragedy in 1980. In a 2007 interview with *W* magazine, DeGeneres described what happened:

> *[Kat and I] had a fight. I left to go stay with friends to try to teach her a lesson. My brother's band was performing. She went looking for me. It was really, really loud, and she was there and she kept saying, "When are you coming back home?" And I kept going, "I can't … I can't hear you. What?"*

I was being really aloof. She kept saying, "Come back home," and then she left. I left a few minutes later, and we passed an accident. The car was split in two …

The next morning her sister came and said, "Kat died last night." And I realized that I had passed it. So I was devastated but just trying to make sense of it. They said she was alive for three hours. Could I have saved her? And why didn't I stop? … I was just talking to her, and if I had said, "Yes, I'll go home with you," she wouldn't have been in that car.[24]

DeGeneres was overwhelmed by her loss, but she again used her gift of humor to help get her through the difficult period. Unable to afford the apartment she had shared with Kat, DeGeneres moved into a small, run-down apartment that was full of fleas. She found herself lying on a mattress on the floor, trying to understand what had happened, as she explained in a 1994 interview:

I'm laying on the floor, wide awake, thinking, "Here's this beautiful girl, 23 years old, who's just gone." So I started writing what it would be like to call God and ask why fleas are here and this person is not. But my mind just kicked into what all of sudden would happen if you actually picked up the phone and called God. How it would take forever, how it would ring for a long time because … it's a big place. And it was like something came through me. I remember writing it nonstop, not thinking what would happen next. And when I finished, I read it and said: "I'm going to do that on Johnny Carson [the host of The Tonight Show *at the time] one day. And he's going to love it. And he's going to invite me to sit on the couch." I knew it was more than funny. I knew it was classic. And it saved me.*[25]

DeGeneres suddenly had a new sense of purpose. She

decided she would continue to pursue comedy. According to a friend, "It took Ellen a long time to get over [Kat's] death, and after she did, it's almost as if Ellen dedicated her success to the woman."[26] Although it was difficult for her to move on, she did not want to spend the rest of her life mourning. She began going out to bars with friends and performing comedy there for extra money, although she was not paid much. While she was perfecting her comedy material, Clyde's Comedy Corner—a comedy club in the busy French Quarter of New Orleans—opened in December 1980. DeGeneres auditioned for Clyde Abercrombie, the owner of the comedy club, and was one of the first people

Clyde's Comedy Corner was in a popular part of New Orleans called the French Quarter, shown here.

he hired. She performed one show a night during the week and two a night on Fridays and Saturdays. She was paid about $300 per week—enough to finally say comedy was her full-time job.

Airing the Truth

In 1981, Betty visited her daughter in New Orleans. She told Ellen that she and B were not getting along, but that she was going to stick it out because the last thing she wanted was another failed marriage. She said she did not have the strength to leave him and go it alone again.

Ellen was visibly disappointed and told Betty that she deserved better than B. Betty tried to defend her husband, so Ellen shared some disturbing news about something B had done to her on more than one occasion when she was a teenager in Texas: He had sexually molested Ellen. The first time occurred soon after Betty's mastectomy.

The two women kept the story to themselves for many more years. However, in 2005, DeGeneres decided to share what happened to her with the public in an interview with *Allure* magazine:

> *Being raised a Christian Scientist, I knew nothing, ironically, about the body. My mother suddenly had an operation for breast cancer. She had a mastectomy. I didn't know anything about breast cancer. I didn't know anything about anything. I was told by my mother's husband that he thinks he feels a lump in her other breast but he doesn't want to alarm her so he needs to feel mine to make sure. He kept insisting he had to see what mine felt like so he could compare. I had no idea that breasts are all different … I knew nothing. A few weeks later, he tried to do it again. And I kept saying, No! No! You can't keep doing this. But it escalated … into other things, until one night when my grandmother was dying and my mother was in New Orleans, I got home after a date … and he tried to break down the door*

to my bedroom. … I had to kick a window out and escape and sleep in a hospital all night long.[27]

DeGeneres admitted that she should have told her mother sooner, but she was trying to protect her mother instead of herself. It was bad enough that her mother had breast cancer, she told herself. She did not want to tell her what horrible things her husband was doing. She thought it would devastate Betty.

Betty confronted B, and he denied it. She was torn; she did not know what to do. She ended up staying with B for several more years, much to Ellen's disappointment, but Ellen forgave her and their strong relationship remained intact.

Another Move

In October 1981, DeGeneres moved to San Francisco, California. The comedy scene was just starting to take off there, so she thought it would be the place to jump-start her career. Clyde's was the only real comedy club in New Orleans, and DeGeneres was hoping that moving somewhere with more options would help her expand her audience. However, since she had not made a name for herself there yet, it was not easy to find work in comedy. Although she loved the atmosphere of San Francisco—especially the thriving LGBT+ community and the increased acceptance—she could not make enough money to support herself with her comedy as she wanted to do. By the summer of 1982, she headed back to New Orleans.

Back in New Orleans, DeGeneres found that Clyde's had closed for good. Although she did get some gigs at other local places, she had to take a job as an office assistant in a law firm to make ends meet. However, DeGeneres did not like her job and admitted she was not very good at it; deep down, she still considered herself a professional comedian.

When cable television became popular in the 1970s,

DeGeneres moved to San Francisco in the 1980s to pursue a stand-up career. Although she loved the city, she could not afford to keep living there.

The late actor Robin Williams, who voiced Genie in Disney's *Aladdin* among many other roles, got his start as a comedian, like DeGeneres. Cable television helped make both of them famous.

channels began giving famous comedians air time. People such as Steve Martin and Robin Williams, both of whom later went on to star in many movies, were able to reach audiences much bigger than any that could possibly fit in a comedy club. However, this also led to an increase in attendance at comedy clubs; people saw some comedians on TV and, when they wanted ed a night out, they would choose to go to comedy clubs to see more. Because the interest in comedy was growing, the cable channel Showtime sponsored a contest for Funniest Person in America. All anyone had to do to audition was send in a tape. DeGeneres knew that if she won, she would instantly make a name for herself as a comedian.

Like the Miss America beauty pageant, the Funniest Person in America contest started with smaller state contests. To win the nationwide title, DeGeneres first had to win the smaller titles, which she did. In *My Point ... and I Do Have One*, DeGeneres explained how she got 1984's Funniest Person in America title:

> The [Funniest Person in New Orleans] contest was at a club before a panel of judges, and about fifteen other people competed, a lot of who had never even been on stage before. I had a 102° fever—I was really, really sick. I almost went home, but I decided to stay. I was the last person on stage, and I won.

> They taped the show that night, and my tape was sent to the contest for the whole state of Louisiana. I won and became the Funniest Person in Louisiana. I don't even think anyone else entered. Then my tape was sent to New York—it was put up in a fine hotel and given one hundred dollars a day spending money, which is a lot for a tape—to compete against tapes from the other forty-nine states. Well, to make a long story short ... my tape, representing Louisiana, made it to the top five from all the states. Then all five tapes went to [comedians] Pee Wee Herman, Harvey Korman, and Soupy Sales—those were the judges—two of whom, if I'm not mistaken, are now on the Supreme Court, and they all picked me as the winner. So I won the Funniest Person in America ... based on that one 102° fever performance.[28]

As the Funniest Person in America, DeGeneres traveled the country at Showtime's expense. She appeared in many comedy clubs and on late-night shows along the way. When she finished the tour, she moved back to San Francisco and started to land stand-up jobs around the country. In doing so, she soon found out how difficult it was to live up to her new title, and she faced her fair share of less-than-welcoming audiences.

DeGeneres still remembers one particularly bad experience in San Francisco, in which she performed for a group of male Marines. The comic who went on before her told

Although DeGeneres had some tough experiences, she did not let them stop her from following her dream as a stand-up comic.

Committed to Clean Comedy

Ever since DeGeneres started doing stand-up comedy, she has never relied on profanity or obscene subject matter to make people laugh. In fact, when Clyde Abercrombie tried to demand that she perform an X-rated show to try to draw in a particular type of audience, DeGeneres told him she would quit rather than make her act dirty. She did not want to limit her audience; she wanted to appeal to all ages. According to Betty DeGeneres, "Many people in the comedy world believe you have to be 'blue' [dirty] to get a laugh, but I think Ellen DeGeneres made them think twice about that."[1]

In an interview with Stone Phillips on *Dateline NBC* on November 8, 2004, DeGeneres talked about her "clean" humor:

> *The reason I do what I do is because I was influenced by Steve Martin, by Woody Allen, by Bob Newhart, by Carol Burnett, by Lucille Ball. I mean, if you put [an obscene word] in front of anything, an audience is going to laugh. You know? It just—it's easy. And I like a challenge.*[2]

1. Betty DeGeneres, *Love, Ellen: A Mother/Daughter Journey*. New York, NY: Rob Weisbach, 1999, pp. 160–161.

2. Quoted in Stone Phillips, "Catching Up with Ellen DeGeneres," *Dateline NBC*, November 8, 2004. www.msnbc.msn.com/id/6430100/print/1/displaymode/1098.

many sexist jokes, which got a lot of laughs from the crowd. When DeGeneres came onstage, instead of listening to her, they shouted sexist comments at her, such as asking her to show them her body. The men in the front row also turned their chairs around so their backs were to her, indicating that they had no interest in her act. DeGeneres dropped the microphone and ran off the stage, but the ordeal was not over yet:

> The emcee felt it necessary to keep emphasizing, "One more time for the Funniest ... Person ... in ... America!" The audience was laughing at him saying it over and over, and I was crying. I wanted to go home and get out of the business. I thought, "This is the worst business; it's so cruel." That was the only time I ever walked off a stage.[29]

Although there were some bad nights, DeGeneres was getting plenty of jobs and was well on her way to building a career in comedy. She started to see that she was learning something from both good and bad audiences.

Without a doubt, her second shot at San Francisco was much more successful than the first. "It was the hottest city there was for comedy, and it was amazing how well things worked there. I really didn't struggle at all. Things just clicked and people started paying attention to me,"[30] she said.

Hitting the Big Time

DeGeneres's next move was to Los Angeles, California, in September 1985. Although she was doing well in San Francisco and working comedy clubs across the country, she had her eye on bigger things. She wanted to work in TV and movies—she wanted to act. She knew Los Angeles was the place to be for that to happen. In 1986, DeGeneres filmed her first HBO special, *The Young Comedians All-Star Reunion*. Then, in 1987 came another, *Women of the Night*. Later in 1986, DeGeneres called her mother and gave her the good news: "November eighteenth, I'm doing *the Tonight Show*! This is it! Johnny Carson!"[31] DeGeneres announced. Back when she was grieving for Kat, when she had written her "A Phone Call to God" routine, DeGeneres knew she would be

Johnny Carson, shown here, changed the lives of many comedians by giving them national exposure.

on Carson's show one day. After all, being on *The Tonight Show* meant a comic had hit the big time. Following a successful appearance, they could expect invitations to be on other shows and to appear all across the country. However, what DeGeneres really wanted was to have Johnny Carson call her over to his couch.

Being called over to talk with Carson was never rehearsed, and no comedian ever knew if they would get the privilege until the moment of truth arrived. If Carson liked what he heard, he would motion the guest to come on over. If he was not impressed, Carson would smile and clap and the show would go to commercial.

A Wish Granted

When the big day came, *The Tonight Show* ran long, and DeGeneres was bumped. She was rescheduled for November 28, Thanksgiving weekend. Betty and other family members gathered together to watch. Betty wrote in *Love, Ellen* about that proud moment:

She got the audience laughing by talking about how mean her parents were to her when she was a kid: "Yeah I remember one day when I was walking home from kindergarten. At least they told me it was kindergarten ... I found out later I'd been working in a factory for two years."

The audience roared, and they roared harder as Ellen said what a healthy, fit family she came from: "When my grandmother was sixty years old she started walking five miles a day. She's ninety-seven now and we don't know where ... she is."

By the time El got into her Phone Call with God, she was being applauded on every line. Amazing.

Gender and Comedy

For decades, a myth has persisted that female comedians are not funny. According to British newspaper *The Guardian*, this is rooted in sexist gender norms:

> *Humour can be very powerful as it shows confidence and great intelligence—and in our culture that is still the male role ... The message to women too often is sadly still "be as attractive to men as possible" and being funny ... loud, aggressive, bossy, ambitious or even nasty just doesn't quite fit that narrative. Women should be pretty. Men should be funny. Most men prefer women to be their appreciative audience, not their competition.*[1]

However, Ellen DeGeneres has proven this myth false with her long, successful career. According to her, she does not think of herself in terms of her gender; she tries to think of herself simply as a comedian, rather than specifically a female comedian. According to one reviewer, because comedy is often still seen as "un-ladylike ... audiences still have to get over their discomfort at having a woman make them laugh at themselves."[2] DeGeneres said, "The comment I hear all the time ... is, 'I don't usually like female comics, but I like you.'"[3]

1. Ayesha Hazarika, "Why Aren't Female Comedians Funny? You Asked Google—Here's the Answer," *The Guardian*, February 1, 2017. www.theguardian.com/commentisfree/2017/feb/01/why-arent-female-comedians-funny-google.

2. Quoted in Kathleen Tracy, *Ellen: The Real Story of Ellen DeGeneres*. Secaucus, NJ: Carol, 1999, p. 71.

3. Quoted in Tracy, *Ellen*, p. 71.

Then something even more amazing happened. After she fin-ished, to thunderous applause, the camera cut over to Johnny. He too was applauding and on his face was the most delighted expression. He raised his hand as if to give her a thumbs-up but suddenly he beckoned her over. Unheard of! Rarely were any comics asked to sit on the panel with Johnny after their first appearance. And never before had any comedienne [female comic] been paneled by Johnny after her debut. So when the camera cut back to Ellen, she stood there with an expression that almost said, "Who me?" Realizing that he meant her, she floated over, smiling radiantly.[32]

On November 28, 1986, Ellen DeGeneres made his-tory. She was the first and only female comedian to be invited to sit on the couch after her first appearance on *The Tonight Show*.

Picking Up Steam

After her appearance on *The Tonight Show*, DeGeneres con-tinued to make strides in her career, appearing on television comedy specials on HBO and ABC and doing other stand-up shows around the country. The more appearances she made and the more popular she became, the more money she could charge for her time.

By this time, Ellen was not the only DeGeneres living in California. Vance, Betty, and Elliott had all moved to the Golden State. Betty had divorced B; she spent a lot of time with her daughter and became one of her greatest supporters, often accompanying her as she traveled to do shows around the country and always in the audience when she performed in town.

In 1989, DeGeneres finally landed a role on a television show, getting a part as a regular on the series *Open House*, which was about a real estate office. She played a secretary-receptionist named Margo Van Meter. The show was canceled in the spring of 1990, but the experience whetted DeGeneres's appetite for more.

After *Open House* was canceled, DeGeneres returned to stand-up comedy. However, now she was performing in theaters, not bars and clubs, which meant people paid admission just to hear her special brand of comedy. She did not have to deal with rude hecklers anymore. In 1990 and 1992, HBO taped two of DeGeneres's performances for its *One Night Stand* comedy special, exposing the comedian to even more fans.

Another sitcom also came DeGeneres's way in 1992. This one, called *Laurie Hill*, had her cast in a small role as nurse Nancy MacIntyre. The show did not get great reviews overall, but many reviewers made special mention of DeGeneres's performance. According to *TV Guide*, DeGeneres as Nancy MacIntyre "provided desperately needed comic relief— and not enough of it."[33] The series was canceled after only five weeks.

Just weeks after learning about *Laurie Hill's* cancellation, DeGeneres signed a deal with ABC to star in her own series, called *These Friends of Mine*. The show would be built around DeGeneres's stand-up persona. She would play Ellen Morgan, an employee of a bookstore called Buy the Book. Each episode would focus on the lives of Morgan and her friends, highlighting the humor in everyday situations. Many critics compared it to comedian Jerry Seinfeld's hit television show *Seinfeld*.

The network ordered 13 episodes and planned to bring it on the air midseason in early 1994. In an interview with the *New York Times*, DeGeneres said, "I was laughing out loud when I read the script. I knew what I could do with it. I wanted to do a smarter, hipper version of *I Love Lucy* … I wanted a show that everybody talks about the next day."[34] In an interview with the *New York Post*, DeGeneres described her television character: "I play this person who's desperate to make everyone happy. Unfortunately, when she does that she ends up putting her foot in her mouth."[35]

DeGeneres finally got to star in her own sitcom in the early 1990s.

Getting Out of the Stand-Up Game

With taping of *These Friends of Mine* scheduled to begin in early 1994, DeGeneres went on a farewell tour, performing for audiences around the country. When asked why she was taking a break from stand-up, DeGeneres said, "I've learned that in life, it's way too important to be happy. If you do something that you're not happy doing—no matter how much you try to fake it—that will eat you up from the inside, that'll kill you."[36]

After *These Friends of Mine* debuted, it ranked third in the ratings and received mixed reviews. When the show was renewed for the 1994 fall season, the name was changed to *Ellen*. However, that was not the only change the show would have over the next few seasons. DeGeneres would indeed explore and learn a lot—about being true to herself, about being a celebrity, and about perseverance. In 1997, DeGeneres proposed a major change to *Ellen* that would affect not only the show but also her career and her personal life.

Chapter Four

A Groundbreaking Episode

Although LGBT+ characters are still underrepresented on television, they were almost never seen before the 21st century, and when they were, they were mainly background characters. Although the TV show *Will & Grace*, which first aired in 1998, featured gay main characters and was a popular sitcom for years, it was *Ellen* that set the stage for normalizing the appearance of LGBT+ people in mainstream media. The show did this with a 1997 episode that is still famous more than 20 years later.

Coming Out to the Public

Ellen was a hit. On the air from 1994 to 1998, the show received good ratings, and DeGeneres received Emmy nominations for her portrayal of Ellen Morgan each season. Life on the set had its ups and downs, however, with several changes over the seasons. In addition to the name change after the first season, the show changed studios and there were cast changes, some of which displeased DeGeneres. However, the ratings remained high, so the show went on.

In 1996, DeGeneres decided it was time to change the show yet again. She approached her mother, Betty, with a decision she had made: She was going to tell the public she was gay. Although today this may seem like no big deal, it was a huge deal back in the mid-1990s. Before DeGeneres came out, actors, actresses, and other celebrities simply were not as open about their sexuality as they are today. As DeGeneres explained later, she was afraid her fans would turn on her if they found out she was gay—that they would never watch her show again or want to see her perform. At the time, coming out meant jeopardizing a career. Many celebrities and entertainment executives feared that once the public knew a celebrity was gay, they would be unable to see past their sexuality and would lose interest or would disapprove due to false ideas about LGBT+ people. The celebrity's opportunities might then dry up. For that reason, many celebrities chose to keep their sexuality a secret.

However, keeping sexual orientation a secret can take a mental toll on someone. It means hiding relationships, choosing words and actions carefully, and always fearing discovery, all of which are stressful. DeGeneres decided she did not want to keep her sexuality a secret any longer—and she was not going to come out alone. She was going to have Ellen Morgan come out too. Since the beginning of the show, there had always been some thought to having Ellen Morgan be gay. The storylines had always left that door open, so it would never seem out of character for her. According to Betty, Ellen did not make this decision impulsively; she had been thinking about it for a long time. She told Betty that she had been in therapy and realized that hiding who she really was had given her a sense of shame. She simply did not want to live like that anymore.

Betty and Ellen discussed the pros and cons of what Ellen was proposing. Betty pointed out that her daughter might risk everything she had worked so hard to attain in her career. She worried about her privacy, although they both admitted that as a star, she no longer had a lot of privacy anyway. Ellen pointed to the many tabloid reports that speculated about her sexuality. Although Betty was worried about what this might mean for her daughter, there was no question that DeGeneres would have her mother's approval and support all the way.

With her mother on her side, DeGeneres next had to convince

DeGeneres decided to come out on her own terms rather than having her secret revealed by the paparazzi.

the executives at ABC and Disney, which owned the network. According to Betty,

> *Ellen knew that even though other TV shows had supporting characters who happened to be gay, there had never been a homosexual lead in a sitcom; she also knew having a lead character go through the process of discovering her or his sexual orientation was something never before done on television. The odds that the network and studio would go for it weren't good. But Ellen had a powerful argument for trying. Grim statistics show that gay teenagers are more at risk of depression, suicide, and attempted suicide, and she felt that this was an opportunity to send a positive message to these kids—as well as to all gay people: "We're OK. We don't have to be ashamed of who we are and who we love."* [37]

DeGeneres approached the studio, and there was a top secret meeting. Her eyes filled with tears as she presented her idea to the writers and producers. It was clear to all in the room just how important this was to her. The response she received was not a yes or a no—it was a maybe. DeGeneres and the other writers would work on a script, but there were no promises that it would ever hit the airwaves.

While the script was in the works, no one wanted any news of the possible storyline to get into the press, so they came up with a code name for the project: "The Puppy Episode." However, by September 1996, as *Ellen* was beginning its fourth season, someone leaked the story. As questions from the media rolled in, the studio simply refused to comment. In the meantime, the writers—including DeGeneres—worked quickly to finish the script.

Filming the Episode

In March 1997, a script for a two-part, hour-long episode in which Ellen Morgan would come out was given approval. By that time, though, many media outlets were already publishing head-

Why Was It Called "The Puppy Episode"?

By the end of the third season of *Ellen*, the producers were becoming increasingly concerned that the show had no real focus and that Ellen Morgan did not show any real interest in the typical sitcom subject matter—relationships and dating. One of the producers suggested that because Morgan was not dating, perhaps she should get a puppy. There was actually some excitement about the idea. However, according to the producers, the idea was really just evidence of how the show had lost its way, that the character had no direction, and that the writers had run of out of good story ideas.

It was soon after the puppy storyline was suggested that DeGeneres approached the network with her proposal that Ellen Morgan come out of the closet. Because of this, when the executives gave the writers the go-ahead to develop a script but wanted to keep it a secret, the episode was nicknamed "The Puppy Episode" in reference to the "Ellen gets a puppy" storyline. The name stuck, and that groundbreaking episode in which Ellen Morgan reveals her sexuality will always be known as "The Puppy Episode."

lines about DeGeneres and the episode, which was still a highly guarded secret. Some—including LGBT+ rights groups—printed favorable articles, but others were negative. DeGeneres, who always practiced good-natured humor and wanted people to like her, had a hard time with the negative press. For example, Jerry Falwell, a pastor and conservative commentator, called her "Ellen Degenerate." In an article in *TIME* magazine, DeGeneres responded, "Really, he called me that? … I've been getting that since the fourth grade. I guess I'm happy I could give him work."[38]

"The Puppy Episode" was shot over two consecutive Fridays.

The shooting of the episode had a definite party atmosphere, with a host of big-name stars making guest appearances, among them Laura Dern as Ellen Morgan's love interest, Oprah Winfrey as her therapist, Demi Moore, and Billy Bob Thornton. Betty DeGeneres also made a cameo, as an extra in the closing scene at an airport.

In the episode, an old male friend from college makes a pass at Ellen Morgan, who comes to realize she is attracted to the friend's female coworker, played by Dern. In the first half of the episode, inside jokes were planted in the script; for instance, at one point, one of the other characters walks into Ellen Morgan's apparently empty apartment, looking for her. After her name is

Because the press had leaked the story of what "The Puppy Episode" was about, the LGBT+ community arranged viewing parties when the episode first aired. They cheered when Ellen Morgan finally said "I'm gay" out loud.

called a few times, Ellen walks out of a door and apologizes for not appearing right away, explaining that she had been in the closet. When Ellen Morgan finally reveals her sexuality, she announces it to an entire airport by accidentally pressing an intercom button as she leans in to whisper it to someone.

Although the studio allowed her to film the episode, there were some things it required that made it clear this was no longer considered a "normal" TV show. For example, starting with "The Puppy Episode," a parental guidance warning appeared before each episode, letting parents know there was adult content in the show. No such warning appeared before other sitcoms, even though *Ellen* never showed more sexual activity than brief kisses.

The Aftermath

Plenty of controversy swirled around the episode both during shooting and after. The worst involved a telephone threat that a bomb had been planted on the set on the last day of shooting. The studio had to be cleared and bomb-sniffing dogs brought in before filming could continue, but no bomb was found. In less violent protests, an ABC affiliate in Birmingham, Alabama, refused to air the episode, and some sponsors—including Chrysler, JCPenney, and Wendy's—pulled their commercials. When hearing about DeGeneres's sexuality, Pat Robertson, a televangelist, said, "I find it hard to believe because she's so popular. She's such an attractive actress."[39] In response, DeGeneres replied, "God, it's weird that somebody popular and attractive can be gay. See, things like that, I don't even have to address those people. They just speak for themselves."[40]

However, the reaction to the coming-out episode was not all negative. LGBT+ groups applauded DeGeneres's courage, even promoting a "Come Out with Ellen" day around the airing of the episode on April 30, 1997.

Immediately following the airing of "The Puppy Episode," *PrimeTime Live*, an ABC news show, aired an interview that DeGeneres and her mother had done with Diane Sawyer. DeGeneres was open and honest about her life and said she realized she might lose both gay and straight fans:

> I'm letting down the straight community that is going to worry about their kids watching me. And I'm letting down the militant gay community that says, "How dare you not be gay enough." But it doesn't mean that I need to be some poster child for anybody …

> For me, this has been the most freeing experience, because people can't hurt me anymore. I don't have to worry about somebody saying something about me or a reporter trying to find out information, because now I'm in control of it … I don't have anything to be scared of, which I think outweighs whatever else happens in my career.[41]

Recognizing the Show

Although there was some negative backlash, the episode received good reviews. An estimated 42 million people watched as *Ellen* made television history, and many of those viewers stuck around to watch the *PrimeTime Live* interview. DeGeneres received other recognition as well. She was given the American Civil Liberties Union (ACLU) Bill of Rights Award; the Jack Benny Award from the University of California, Los Angeles; and the Stephen F. Kolzak Award from LGBT+ rights group GLAAD. She also topped many of the year's "Most Fascinating" and "Most Influential" lists. In her acceptance speech for the ACLU Bill of Rights Award, DeGeneres said,

> I feel like I'm being honored for helping myself. I had no idea how many other lives would be affected by what I've done …

> I got to a place where I needed to live my life freely. I didn't want to feel ashamed of who I was anymore. Thank God, literally, thank God for allowing me to get there. Some people never do.

Being true to herself has always been important to DeGeneres, and she encourages others to do the same.

Some people hide a little bit of who they are because it's safer in this world to hide than to be yourself. Rather than celebrate individuality, society would rather have others feel uncomfortable and stay quiet, or better yet, be invisible …

How sad. I feel overwhelmed sometimes. And I feel a responsibility to continue to simply be myself. I want to continue acting, entertaining, making people laugh, making people feel good. And I will also dedicate my life to making it safe for all people to live

An Actress, A Comic, and an Author

In addition to being a stand-up comic, talk-show host, and actress, Ellen DeGeneres is also a best-selling author. Her first book, *My Point … and I Do Have One*, came out in 1995, debuting at the number 1 spot on the *New York Times* best seller list.

When the publisher first approached DeGeneres about writing a book, the hope was that she would write an autobiography. However, she was not interested in that. She wanted to write a comedy book, and that is what it became. DeGeneres followed up her first book with a second, *The Funny Thing Is …*, in 2003. DeGeneres showcased her subtle humor on the book's jacket: "DeGeneres takes an innovative approach to the organization of her book by utilizing a section in the beginning that includes the name of each chapter, along with a corresponding page number. She calls it the 'Table of Contents,' and she is confident that it will become the standard to which all books in the future will aspire."[1]

1. Ellen DeGeneres, *The Funny Thing Is …* New York, NY: Simon & Schuster, 2003, book jacket copy.

their lives freely—whatever that means.[42]

Months later, DeGeneres was nominated for two Emmy Awards for "The Puppy Episode": one for Outstanding Lead Actress in a Comedy Series and the other for Outstanding Writing for a Comedy Series. DeGeneres lost out to Helen Hunt for the first award, but she won the second. In her acceptance speech, she said, "I accept this on behalf of all the people, and the teenagers especially, out there who think there's something wrong with them because they're gay. Don't ever let anybody make you feel ashamed of who you are."[43]

Coming Out Again

Around the same time Ellen Morgan came out on television, Ellen DeGeneres officially came out too, with an appearance on the cover of *TIME* magazine in April 1997 with the funny title, "Yep, I'm Gay." In the interview, she talked about how stressful her life had been when she felt she had a big secret to keep:

> *I always thought I could keep my personal life separate from my professional life … In every interview I ever did … everyone tried to trap me into saying I was gay. And I learned every way to dodge that. Or if they just blatantly asked me, I would say I don't talk about my personal life. I mean, I really tried to figure out every way to avoid answering that question for as long as I could.*[44]

Over the next several months, DeGeneres and her mother received hundreds of letters from LGBT+ men and women and their family members, thanking them for their courage and relaying their own stories of how they had been discriminated against or accepted by friends, parents, and society. Many men and women recounted how "The Puppy Episode" had given them the courage to come out; other letters were from parents who had changed their views toward their own LGBT+ children thanks to Betty's example of love and acceptance. However, they had their fair share of hate mail as well—either directly or through the media.

In a 2004 interview with Stone Phillips on *Dateline NBC*, DeGeneres was asked about her decision to come out. She replied,

> When I made the decision to come out, everything was great. And I really naively thought nobody's going to care, you know. It's like, I'm going to just now say, by the way, I'm gay. I mean, all of my business people, all my people, were saying, don't do it, you know … I couldn't listen to them. I had to listen to me. You know? It's my life. It's my heart. It's my soul. It's my journey. And it's who I am.[45]

DeGeneres's Dating Life

Now openly out, DeGeneres found that the public's fascination with her personal life only grew, especially since she had admitted during the Diane Sawyer interview that she was in a relationship. Because she had been spotted with actress Anne Heche, speculation grew that she was DeGeneres's girlfriend. Most people believed Heche to be heterosexual, so the story grabbed the public's attention and ignited a media firestorm.

As it turned out, DeGeneres and Heche had met at an Oscar party on March 24, 1997. They soon fell in love. Due to the rumors surrounding their relationship, in April 1997, DeGeneres and Heche appeared on *Oprah* and admitted they were dating. They wanted to address the public's reaction. They shared with the talk-show host that they felt stigmatized by the media and the entertainment industry for their decision to come out. They thought it was negatively affecting their work lives. The two also spoke of being together forever.

The Effect on Ellen

Ellen was renewed for a fifth season, but it would be its last. Going forward, the show explored storylines that followed Ellen

One of DeGeneres's most public relationships was with actress Anne Heche (right).

Morgan as a single gay woman dating different women and sometimes forming relationships. As time went on, DeGeneres and the show's executives were often at odds over storylines and how episodes should be rated, and some advertisers and organized groups still had trouble with the gay content of the show. Rumors swirled about problems on the set and that the show would be canceled. Even with all the negative press, most critics were still giving it good reviews; however, after "The Puppy Episode," the executives promoted the show less, which led to fewer people watching it. In turn, this caused a drop in ratings that gave the executives an excuse to cancel the show. Robert Iger, who was the president of ABC at the time, stated that it was not because of DeGeneres's personal life; in an interview with Diane Sawyer, he said, "It became a program about a lead character who was gay every single week. I just think that was too much for some people." In response, Sawyer said, "Well, she *is* gay every single week, though,"[46] highlighting the fact that DeGeneres's sexuality was not simply a way of acting—it was part of who she was. DeGeneres admitted, however, that the drop in ratings may have been partially because she tried to use the show to tackle important issues that often come up when someone comes out. She said, "I tried to incorporate educational things about what people actually go through when they're coming out, and it wasn't funny … Because it's not funny."[47] When a show that people associate with nonstop humor starts to get serious, some people choose to stop watching, even if the quality of the show has not declined.

Ellen was canceled in the spring of 1998. DeGeneres was incredibly hurt, but she worked to end the show on a high note. The last episode was a mockumentary, as DeGeneres referred to it, of her career and the history of television. Again the episode featured an all-star cast, including Glenn Close, Cindy Crawford, Helen Hunt, Ted Danson, Woody Harrelson, and Linda Ellerbee as the interviewer. The episode was shot over several days, and throughout the process of ending the show, DeGeneres was very emotional.

For DeGeneres, things seemed to go from bad to worse. Although everything seemed to be fine between her and Heche, on August 19, 2000, the couple made a public announcement that they were ending their relationship of three and a half years. Later that same day, Heche knocked on a stranger's door in Fresno, California, took a shower, and settled in to watch a movie. When there was no sign that she was going to leave, the police were called. Heche was briefly hospitalized and then released. After a messy breakup, Heche married a cameraman who had been with the couple on a trip to film DeGeneres's stand-up comedy. The breakup hit DeGeneres hard, as she explained to a reporter for the *Advocate*, a LGBT+ monthly newsmagazine:

> *It feels like your sides are cracking open. I hadn't experienced it before. I had never been left by anybody—I was always the one to leave ... And it feels like you cannot go on. And I would sit and literally not know where the day went. The sun would come up and the sun would go down, and I didn't notice because I was just staring at the wall. I didn't leave my house. I would go through days of crying. It felt like I would never live again. But you do.*[48]

DeGeneres had hit a rough patch in her life, both personally and professionally. She believed her very public breakup with Heche had eaten away at the goodwill her fans had felt for her after she announced she was a lesbian. In an article in *People* magazine, she said, "I went through a phase, whether it was true or not, where my perception was, 'Everyone hates me now,' and it felt horrible."[49]

Throughout her life, DeGeneres has endured all kinds of adversity. One thing that had always gotten her through the toughest times was her special brand of humor—her ability to make people laugh and to point out the silliness in everyday situations. Now, however, she was facing the most difficult challenges of her life, and it was a struggle for her to pick herself up and move on.

Chapter Five

The Star of the Show

After *Ellen* was canceled in the wake of "The Puppy Episode," DeGeneres feared her career was over. On top of that, she was dealing with the stress and heartbreak of the end of her relationship with Anne Heche. However, just as she had not given up when things got tough in the past, DeGeneres picked up the pieces of her life and kept moving forward. Her hard work and determination paid off, and today, she is a major celebrity with several projects in the works, the best known of which is her popular talk show, *The Ellen DeGeneres Show*.

Picking Up the Pieces

After her very public breakup with Heche, DeGeneres did not hide out for long. Instead, she got back to work. In a 2005 interview with *Allure* magazine, DeGeneres reflected on what happened after the breakup:

> Anne broke my heart into a million pieces, I've never spoken to her since she left … When Anne left, I'd wake up in the

morning, and my eyes would just immediately fill up with tears, and I would start convulsively crying. I'd watch the sun come up and then go down, and I'd literally be in the same place on the floor. I finally just thought, I'm not going to let this destroy me. I'm so grateful for it, finally. I think everybody needs to have their heart broken.[50]

DeGeneres decided to get back to where it all started for her—doing stand-up comedy. She wrote a routine called *The Beginning*, which was recorded for HBO and aired in 2000. The special was later nominated for two Emmy Awards.

In 2001, DeGeneres was approached with an idea to do a variety show. That idea eventually turned into another sitcom, this one about a gay woman who moves to a small town from a big city. *The Ellen Show* was not a hit with audiences or reviewers, however, and although 18 episodes had been recorded, only 13 were ever aired. The show was canceled after one season. In that same year, though, DeGeneres began what many have referred to as her second act. In an interview with Guy MacPherson of the website Comedy Couch, DeGeneres talked about the cancellation:

I don't think it was really given a chance. But I think it had potential. I feel like it fell kind of in the middle. It was neither/nor. It either should have been a little bit edgier and smarter or ... It just kind of ... You know, I'm never going to get the Everybody Loves Raymond audience. I'm not going to get the families. I think there are people that are still unfortunately still holding on to some old baggage. I think I'll get them. I think people will kind of let go of all that, and if something's funny and if something's good, they will come back eventually.[51]

Laughter After Tragedy

Soon after the terrorist attacks of September 11, 2001, DeGeneres was asked to host the Primetime Emmy Awards. She accepted, hoping her appearance would win some support for *The Ellen Show*. The awards show was delayed twice, however, because of the country's situation. Many people simply felt the American people were not yet ready to laugh, and what is often a fancy celebration seemed so trivial in light of what had just happened. The entire entertainment industry was struggling with how to amuse audiences without appearing insensitive. Many thought maybe they should not even try. However, they underestimated the power of DeGeneres's humor. After all, her wit had been helping her and her mother through hard times for years.

DeGeneres impressed the nation—including her colleagues in attendance and millions of television viewers—with her performance. She even received a standing ovation from her audience. Following the show, *People* magazine printed a recap: "Forget the quiet tributes and subtle protests. Stepping onstage at L.A.'s Shubert Theater on Nov. 4 ... host Ellen DeGeneres set the forthright tone: 'What would bug the Taliban more than seeing a gay woman in a suit surrounded by Jews?'"[52] *Entertainment Weekly* described the comedian's performance as "witty, respectful, and wise."[53]

Although her sitcom did not do well, over the next year, DeGeneres was appearing on television more and more, both as herself and in character. She hosted *Saturday Night Live*, made a guest appearance on an episode of the hit sitcom *Will & Grace*, and took center square on the game show *Hollywood Squares*. It seemed the public wanted to see more of DeGeneres, and soon it would get exactly that.

An Exciting Proposal

In 2003, DeGeneres was offered a great opportunity: her own daytime talk show. She agreed to do it. However, a talk show takes time to develop, so while *The Ellen DeGeneres Show* was

After September 11, 2001, DeGeneres hosted the Emmy Awards, which helped get her career back on track.

in the works, DeGeneres wrote a new stand-up routine, toured the country with it, and filmed a New York performance for an HBO special called *Ellen DeGeneres: Here and Now*. Bret Fetzer of the website Amazon reviewed her performance when the show came out on DVD:

> With a loose, free-associative flow, Ellen DeGeneres glides through her 2003 HBO special, Here and Now … Her genius is that she never seems like a genius; on the contrary, DeGeneres seems like your next-door neighbor pointing out the obvious, yet somehow an hour whizzes by in complete enjoyment. It's peerless observational humor—nothing groundbreaking or piercingly satirical, but simply fun.[54]

DeGeneres also wrote a second book of essays, *The Funny Thing Is* …, which, like her first book, became an instant best seller. A review of the book's audio version in *Publisher's Weekly* said,

> The laid-back, observational comedienne's stream-of-[consciousness] musings gain additional zest from her wry and adroit delivery. Some of her funniest material is in throw-away lines, dropped with an easygoing deadpan delivery. ("My

In 2003, DeGeneres wrote her second book, entitled *The Funny Thing Is ...*

favorite exercise is walking a block and a half to the corner store to buy fudge. Then I call a cab to get back home. There's never a need to overdo anything.") Her smart and funny routines point out absurdities in everyday life. ("Batteries are packaged as though the manufacturers never want you to get to them. On the other hand, take a good look at a package of light bulbs. Thin, thin, thin cardboard that's open on both ends.") Whether offering tips to cover social embarrassments or grousing about parallel parking ("What better way to do something you're already a little leery about doing than by doing it backwards?"), DeGeneres is a delight.[55]

Live-Action Films

Many people are well aware of DeGeneres's role as Dory, a fish with short-term memory loss, in the Disney/Pixar hit movies *Finding Nemo* and *Finding Dory*. She also lent her voice to one of the animals in *Doctor Doolittle*, starring Eddie Murphy, and she played herself on an episode of *The Simpsons* in 2010—a sure sign that she had become a household name. She also played herself on an episode of *The Big Bang Theory* in 2016. However, DeGeneres has also appeared in a number of live-action films, most of which were not widely publicized but did give her favorable reviews.

In 1996, DeGeneres starred with Bill Pullman in the movie *Mr. Wrong*, which is about a woman on a quest to find Mr. Right. When she thinks she has finally found him, he turns out to be all wrong; DeGeneres's character tries to break up with him, and mayhem ensues. Many reviewers disliked the movie, but they had better things to say about DeGeneres's performance. The *Boston Herald* reviewer, for example, said that DeGeneres was

Voicing a Fish

Also in 2003, DeGeneres made a big splash when she lent her voice to the character Dory, a lovable and comically forgetful blue tang fish, in Disney/Pixar's animated movie *Finding Nemo*. The part was written with DeGeneres in mind, and both audiences and critics alike loved her in the role.

Andrew Stanton, *Finding Nemo*'s director and cowriter, explained to *Entertainment Weekly* why he wrote the part for DeGeneres: "Everybody has that friend who's funny merely for existing. That's Ellen. You're not waiting for a punchline with her. You're just waiting for her to speak so you can start

DeGeneres is shown here in the 1999 film *Edtv*.

an appealing comic heroine. DeGeneres also appeared as television producer Cynthia Topping in the Ron Howard–directed movie *Edtv* in 1999. Her other movies include 1998's *Goodbye Lover*, 1999's *The Love Letter*, and 2001's *Reaching Normal*.

laughing."[56] In 2004, DeGeneres was given the Nickelodeon Kids' Choice Award for Favorite Voice from an Animated Movie for her performance. In 2016, she received the same award from the Kids' Choice Awards for voicing Dory in *Finding Dory*.

In an interview for CBS's *Early Show* to promote *Finding Nemo*, Laurie Hibberd asked DeGeneres if there had ever been a time when all that she had going for her—a successful movie, a book, an HBO comedy special—never seemed possible. DeGeneres replied,

"I'm an example that you shouldn't give up … That no matter how bleak something looks, you shouldn't give up." She said

One of DeGeneres's best-known and best-loved roles is Dory the fish, which earned her multiple Kids' Choice Awards.

after her last HBO special, "The Beginning" … she stopped hearing the phone ring for work and wasn't being hired for anything. "I just decided, 'This is crazy' … I hadn't done stand-up in 8 years because I had had a television show, and when that got canceled, I just thought I'd go back to how I started. I'll go back to the beginning … I just kept walking, I just kept moving. Or as Dory would say, 'I just kept swimming' … I just really feel like no matter what, you just keep going. And if you're doing something from a place of truth, it can't hurt you."[57]

A Hit Talk Show

In the fall of 2003, *The Ellen DeGeneres Show* finally hit the airwaves. In its first season, it earned good reviews and solid ratings across the country. The show was so well received, in fact, that in 2004, it was nominated for a record-setting 12 Daytime Emmy Awards—the most for any daytime talk show in its debut season. When DeGeneres learned of the nominations, she responded, "They told me, you got nominations for every single category except the song, and I instantly said, 'What's wrong with our song?'"[58] The show ended up winning three technical awards and the award for Outstanding Talk Show.

In an interview with Stone Phillips on *Dateline NBC*, DeGeneres spoke about her daytime talk show: "I'll do anything for a laugh. I love the show. I love doing it. I get so much from it. It's an amazing thing that I lost everything from being me and then I'm now just being me and it feels good on many, many levels."[59]

Each year, *The Ellen DeGeneres Show* wins more awards, and each day, it gets an audience of about 2.9 million viewers. As of early 2018, the show has won a total of 10 Daytime Emmy Awards—the most of any talk show in Daytime Emmy history. In early 2009, DeGeneres celebrated her 1,000th episode, and in 2014, after she hosted the Oscars, her show broke its old record for highest ratings with 4.8 million viewers.

In addition to her numerous Daytime Emmys, DeGeneres has made history by winning 20 People's Choice Awards as of 2017—the most ever won by one person. She was voted Best Daytime Talk Show Host by *Parade* readers and Favorite TV Personality by the Harris Poll's annual favorite television star list, beating Oprah Winfrey and Jay Leno. DeGeneres was also included in MSNBC's "Power Players Who Shape Your TV Habits." She topped the list of Oxygen's "50 Funniest Women Alive," which also included comedic greats Carol Burnett and Lily Tomlin. DeGeneres has also been included in *TIME* magazine's "100 Most Influential People" list, and in 2009, DeGeneres was named the most powerful gay celebrity by *Out* magazine.

DeGeneres has received numerous other awards and honorable mentions over the years, but perhaps the most distinguished award she has received is the Presidential

DeGeneres set a record for the most People's Choice Awards ever to be won by a single person. All 20 of them are shown in this photo from the 2017 awards ceremony.

Medal of Freedom, which President Barack Obama gave her in 2016. This award, according to Obama, "is not just our nation's highest civilian honor—it's a tribute to the idea that all of us, no matter where we come from, have the opportunity to change this country for the better."[60] It is presented to people who have made significant contributions to the United States. According to a White House press release, DeGeneres was given the award because "In her work and in her life, she has been a passionate advocate for equality and fairness."[61]

That Special Something

So what makes DeGeneres's show so popular? Other comedians have tried talk shows, but few have been as popular with both stars and audiences alike. For one thing, the show offers a unique mix of interviews with Hollywood stars, performances by popular and up-and-coming musical guests, silly audience participation games, and spotlights on everyday people who have special talents or who have done amazing things. When DeGeneres sees someone with a special talent, she wants them on the show. DeGeneres encourages a negativity-free zone on her show and has created an atmosphere where everybody feels they are in the studio—even those watching from home. She even created a "Riff Raff Room," where people who stood in line but did not get tickets to that day's show can sit and still feel a part of the show. To make viewers part of the show, DeGeneres often makes phone calls and encourages everyone to send in videos and letters, which she frequently shares on the air.

Aside from DeGeneres's unique brand of comedy, one of the greatest trademarks of the show is the dancing. In 2004, when Stone Phillips asked why the audience dances even though they are not told they have to, DeGeneres replied,

> Well, it just happens because I dance. Nobody dances anymore. Unless you're, you know, like 18 through your 20s and you go to clubs, you stop going out and you stop dancing. So these people come, and they're anywhere from 16 years old to 80 years old. And they're all dancing. And it feels good.[62]

Additionally, DeGeneres attracts celebrities to her show by being kind—something fairly rare in show business, where many celebrities who go on talk shows are asked about their most painful and private moments. DeGeneres has always made it clear that she is not out to make anyone feel bad, even if it would boost her ratings. After singer Katy Perry's divorce from Russell Brand after only 14 months, she went

DeGeneres loves to dance, and her guests, including Michelle Obama (left), often dance with her.

on *The Ellen DeGeneres Show* and, instead of talking about her painful experience, spoke to DeGeneres about her work before playing a game of Taboo with her.

Being herself has also helped DeGeneres get people to be more accepting of homosexuality. She is popular even with people who have voted for politicians who oppose it, possibly because she has shown them that she is a regular person like them. When she went on a nationwide tour before premiering her talk show, she recalled, "They were always shocked. They'd be like, 'She didn't curse,' as though cursing were a characteristic of gay people."[63]

The Real Thing

DeGeneres starting dating photographer Alexandra Hedison in 2001. In 2004, while still with Hedison, DeGeneres appeared on *Dateline NBC*. Phillips asked DeGeneres if she was surprised that in 2004, sexual orientation and gay marriage were still such hot-button issues in the United States. DeGeneres replied,

Am I surprised? No. No. You know, I wish that I wasn't seen differently. I wish that people looked at me and just saw that I was a good person with a good heart. And that wants to make people laugh. And that's who I am. I also happen to be gay. And I would love to have the same rights as everybody else. I would love, I don't care if it's called marriage, I don't care if it's called, you know, domestic partnership. I don't care what it's called. I mean, there are couples that have been together, 30 years, 40 years. And all of a sudden, they lose their house, you know, because the taxes kill them, because it's different because they're not married. Everything is taken away just because. You know, with Sept. 11, there are a lot of people that lost their partner and didn't get the same benefits. It's not fair. And at the same time I know there are people watching right now saying, you know, it's sick it's wrong, it's this. And it's like, convince them that I'm not sick or wrong, that there's nothing wrong with me. You know, I can live my life and hope that things change, and hope that we're protected as any other couples.[64]

When the relationship with Hedison ended in late 2004, DeGeneres started to date Australian-born actress Portia de Rossi, who has starred in television shows such as *Arrested Development* and *Ally McBeal*. According to de Rossi in a 2009 interview, she had actually met DeGeneres in 2000 but had not come out yet and was too nervous to approach her. They moved in together soon after they started dating; in 2005, they began wearing matching rings to signify that they considered themselves married, even though they could not make it legal. However, when the California state supreme court legalized

DeGeneres and de Rossi have been happily married since 2008, although they considered themselves married even before it was legal.

gay marriage in 2008, the two were married on August 16, 2008, in a small ceremony at their home in California. Soon after they were married, however, gay marriage was banned once again in California with the passage of Proposition 8 during the November election.

In an interview, DeGeneres reacted to the ban, saying she was "saddened beyond belief" and that she, "like millions of Americans, felt like we had taken a giant step toward equality" by electing Barack Obama as president, but with the passage of Proposition 8, "we took a giant step away." DeGeneres had donated money to help fight the ban and said she would "continue to speak out for equality for all of us."[65] In 2015, the U.S. Supreme Court ruled that same-sex marriage was legal throughout the United States.

The couple celebrated their ninth anniversary in 2017 and made posts on social media declaring how happy they were together—and still very much in love. For DeGeneres's 60th birthday in January 2018, de Rossi surprised her with a gift that proves she truly understands her wife. She opened the Ellen DeGeneres Campus of the Dian Fossey Gorilla Fund to help carry on the work of the late Dian Fossey—one of DeGeneres's heroes—a researcher who was known for working to save mountain gorillas in Rwanda. Additionally, de Rossi created the Ellen DeGeneres Wildlife Fund to help DeGeneres raise money to help endangered species around the globe. DeGeneres called it the best gift she has ever received.

The couple has no children and does not plan to adopt any. As de Rossi said, "You have to really want kids, and neither of us did."[66] Instead, they adopted several pets, including a dog they named Kid as a joke about the number of times they have been asked when they will adopt a kid.

Branching Out

Today, DeGeneres is involved in so much more than her successful talk show. For example, in August 2009, *American Idol* judge Paula Abdul, a fan favorite, left the wildly popular TV

Showing Her Love
for Animals

Today Ellen DeGeneres and Portia de Rossi have many pets, including cats and dogs. She and de Rossi have also been vegans for years, which means they eat no animal products, including eggs, cheese, and honey. In 2009, People for the Ethical Treatment of Animals (PETA) named DeGeneres its Woman of the Year. DeGeneres designs a line of pet products that is sold at PetSmart and even co-owns a brand of holistic pet care products called Halo. It includes all-natural dog and cat foods, supplements, treats, and grooming supplies.

There is some controversy surrounding Halo—specifically, its sale of vegan dog food. Some people approve of this type of dog food because they believe it is cruel to allow some animals to be killed to feed other animals. However, others say a vegan diet is unhealthy for dogs. According to veterinarian Dr. Karen Becker, "Dogs are scavenging carnivores. In general terms this means they are primarily meat-eaters, but can survive on plant material alone if necessary. The key word here is 'survive' ... To thrive is to grow vigorously ... To survive means simply to stay alive."[1] In other words, while a dog may not die if it is fed only vegan food, it will likely not be very healthy.

1. Karen Becker, "The Alarming New Vegan Pet Food Branded by Celebrity Ellen DeGeneres," Healthy Pets, January 19, 2012. healthypets.mercola.com/sites/healthypets/archive/2012/01/19/vegetarianism-for-pets.aspx.

show. Of *American Idol*'s four judges, Abdul had been viewed as the kindest in her critiques of contestants' performances. On September 10, 2009, the Fox network announced that they had asked DeGeneres to replace Abdul and that DeGeneres had accepted. It was expected that, like Abdul, the comedian would be a gentle judge.

In the media storm that followed, fans appeared thrilled with the development. However, critics pointed out that, unlike professional singer and dancer Abdul, DeGeneres has had no music experience. Many questioned her ability to be an effective judge. DeGeneres also quickly found that it was too hard for her to pass judgment on people who were trying their hardest; she did not want to hurt anyone's feelings. She left the show only months later and admitted in 2015 that it had been a mistake to agree to it.

In 2017, DeGeneres began hosting her own game show: *Ellen's Game of Games*. However, DeGeneres has not limited her talent to appearing on television. She has also gone behind the scenes, creating a production company called A Very Good Production, Inc. One of its projects is a nonfiction series called *Little Funny* that follows 11-year-old Saffron Herndon as she practices her stand-up comedy. DeGeneres expressed admiration for the child comedian, saying, "It's crazy that Saffy is telling such hilarious jokes at 11 years old. When I was 11, I was telling knock-knock jokes. To be honest, I'm still telling knock-knock jokes."[67] As of early 2018, the series is still in development.

In 2011, DeGeneres also cofounded a record label called eleveneleven, a name she chose because she felt the number had significance for her. Many people, DeGeneres included, say that they see the time 11:11 on clocks more frequently than other times, and some believe it is a time when people can make a wish that will come true later. Additionally, when she found the first singer for her record label—Greyson Chance—she found him on the 11th of the month and his soccer jersey number was 11, so she felt it was another sign.

Just how long *The Ellen DeGeneres Show* will last is anybody's guess. In an interview with Judith Newman for *Ladies' Home Journal*, she said the end could be 10 years down the road: "I don't need to be on camera. I'm not a workaholic. I love to spend time with my wife, my family, my animals. We're looking for the right place to have a farm. Someplace like Massachusetts or Nantucket, with seasons. We could get an 1800s farmhouse with land and rescue animals. Then I'm

A Celebrity Philanthropist

DeGeneres has been praised for being a philanthropist, or someone who gives large amounts of money to charities and other good causes. In August 2017, right after Hurricane Harvey made landfall in Texas, the online magazine *SheKnows* ran an article about some of DeGeneres's good deeds:

> *We were reminded of just how charitable DeGeneres is this week when she pledged to donate upward of $75,000 to humans and animals impacted by the devastation of Hurricane Harvey ...*
>
> *And this is hardly the first time DeGeneres has lent a hand.*
>
> *DeGeneres (who was honored as the People's Choice Awards' Favorite Humanitarian last year) has given away way more than $50 million dollars on her show. She has raised $12.5 million for breast cancer, more than $10 million for families affected by Hurricane Katrina and more*

done."[68] That was in 2009, but as of early 2018, DeGeneres has given no indication that she is close to retirement. Additionally, although she stated in that interview that she and de Rossi are simply looking for a place to settle down, DeGeneres has gained a reputation for buying and selling houses. Some people believe she is a house flipper, or someone who buys houses to renovate and resell. Between 2007 and 2017, she owned and sold at least seven homes, and she often completely redecorates them before selling them. However, DeGeneres has said, "I've never bought to sell. I always say: 'This is it. I'm never moving.' People laugh at me now."[69]

Finding Her Place

With a successful talk show, awards almost too numerous to

than $21 million to individuals and families who shared their stories with her. DeGeneres has even inspired her audience to donate more than $35 million of their own. And that's just the tip of the iceberg.[1]

In February 2018, DeGeneres gave away her biggest single gift to date: She partnered with Cheerios cereal to give the studio audience at one of her shows $1 million to split. The gift was a celebration of her 60th birthday as well as an attempt to reward love and kindness. DeGeneres said, "This audience is filled with people who are making a difference in the world by sharing good ... This is the biggest gift I've ever given anybody ever. And I hope you continue to pay it forward and share all the good."[2]

1. Cooper Lawrence, "Here's Why Ellen DeGeneres Just Might Be the Most Charitable Person Alive," *SheKnows*, August 29, 2017. www.sheknows.com/entertainment/articles/1108319/times-ellen-degeneres-charitable-giving-changed-lives.

2. Quoted in Julia Curley, "Ellen DeGeneres Shocked Fans with Her Biggest Audience Gift Ever," *Today*, February 3, 2018. www.today.com/popculture/see-ellen-degeneres-shock-her-fans-biggest-audience-gift-ever-t122210.

count, two best-selling books, several side projects, and a happy marriage, Ellen DeGeneres has come a long way from the drama that surrounded her coming out in 1997.

In 2004, while promoting *Finding Nemo*, she told Stone Phillips,

It's amazing to me that I have achieved what I've achieved.

Nothing has been easy. Not one step of the way has been easy. I'm really proud that I am strong, because I didn't think I was strong. And I think when you bring up Dory, you know, there's that moment in the movie when he's saying, you know, goodbye to her. And she starts crying and says, I feel like I'm home. That's what I feel like. I feel like I am finally home with everything.[70]

Notes

Chapter One: Early Life

1. Ellen DeGeneres, *My Point … and I Do Have One*. New York, NY: Bantam Books, 1995, "Thanks for No Memory."

2. Betty DeGeneres, *Love, Ellen: A Mother/Daughter Journey*. New York, NY: Rob Weisbach, 1999, pp. 71–72.

3. DeGeneres, *My Point*, p. 128.

4. Quoted in Dotson Rader, "Ellen DeGeneres Talks Feelings, Fun, and *Finding Dory*," *Parade*, June 10, 2016. parade.com/482237/dotsonrader/ellen-degeneres-talks-feelings-fun-and-finding-dory/.

5. Quoted in Kathleen Tracy, *Ellen: The Real Story of Ellen DeGeneres*. Secaucus, NJ: Carol, 1999, p. 8.

6. DeGeneres, *Love, Ellen*, pp. 100–102.

7. Quoted in Rader, "Ellen DeGeneres Talks Feelings."

8. DeGeneres, *My Point*, p. 201.

9. Quoted in Tracy, *Ellen*, p. 13.

10. Quoted in DeGeneres, *Love, Ellen*, pp. 115–116.

11. Quoted in Tracy, *Ellen*, p. 17.

12. DeGeneres, *Love, Ellen*, pp. 120–121.

13. Quoted in William Keck, "DeGeneres on a Mission: Breast Cancer Awareness," *USA Today*, September 30, 2007. www.usatoday.com/life/people/2007-09-26-ellen-de generes_N.htm.

14. DeGeneres, *Love, Ellen*, "Atlanta, Texas."

15. DeGeneres, *Love, Ellen*, p. 119.

Chapter Two: Getting Her Start

16. DeGeneres, *Love, Ellen*, p. 129.

17. Quoted in Stone Phillips, "Catching Up with Ellen DeGeneres," *Dateline NBC*, November 8, 2004. www.msnbc.msn.com/id/6430100/print/1/display-mode/1098.

18. DeGeneres, *Love, Ellen*, p. 129.

19. DeGeneres, *Love, Ellen*, p. 139.

20. Quoted in Tracy, *Ellen*, p. 32.

21. Quoted in Tracy, *Ellen*, p. 32.

22. Quoted in Tracy, *Ellen*, p. 35.

23. DeGeneres, *Love, Ellen*, p. 158.

Chapter Three: A Brave Woman

24. Quoted in Bridget Foley, "Ellen DeGeneres," *W*, March 1, 2007. www.wmagazine.com/story/ellen-degeneres.

25. Quoted in Bill Carter, "At Lunch With: Ellen DeGeneres; Dialed God (Pause). He Laughed," *New York Times*, April 13, 1994, p. C1.

26. Quoted in Tracy, *Ellen*, p. 38.

27. Quoted in Kevin Sessums, "Mother Nature," *Allure*, June 1, 2005, p. 194.

28. DeGeneres, *My Point*, pp. 29–31.

29. Quoted in Tracy, *Ellen*, p. 52.

30. Quoted in Tracy, *Ellen*, p. 52.

31. Quoted in DeGeneres, *Love, Ellen*, p. 191.

32. DeGeneres, *Love, Ellen*, p. 193.

33. Quoted in Tracy, *Ellen*, p. 74.

34. Quoted in Carter, "At Lunch With," p. C1.

35. Quoted in Tracy, *Ellen*, p. 84.

36. Quoted in DeGeneres, *Love, Ellen*, p. 223.

Chapter Four: A Groundbreaking Episode

37. DeGeneres, *Love, Ellen*, p. 242.

38. Quoted in DeGeneres, *Love, Ellen*, p. 244.

39. Quoted in Tracy, *Ellen*, p. 209.

40. Quoted in Tracy, *Ellen*, p. 209.

41. Quoted in Tracy, *Ellen*, p. 207.

42. Quoted in DeGeneres, *Love, Ellen*, pp. 261–262.

43. Quoted in Tracy, *Ellen*, p. 242.

44. Quoted in Bruce Handy, "Roll Over, Ward Cleaver," *TIME*, April 14, 1997. www.time.com/time/print-out/0,8816,986 188,00.html.

45. Quoted in Phillips, "Catching Up with Ellen DeGeneres."

46. "Ellen: Uncesored—Primetime Live 1998," YouTube video, 17:43, posted by lolluzza91, April 2, 2013. www.youtube.com/watch?v=Y9HsdLZ6q1A.

47. Quoted in Sarah Karlan, "23 Things You Didn't Know About the 'Ellen' Sitcom," BuzzFeed,

March 29, 2014. www.buzzfeed.com/skarlan/23-things-you-didnt-know-about-the-ellen-sitcom?utm_term=.dbPeq4Y3j#.bbkV8D2Pq.

48. Quoted in Judy Wieder, "Ellen Again," *Advocate*, September 25, 2001, p. 58.

49. Quoted in Notable Biographies, "Ellen DeGeneres Biography," *Encyclopedia of World Biography*. www.notablebiographies.com/news/Ca-Ge/DeGeneres-Ellen.html.

Chapter Five: The Star of the Show

50. Quoted in Sessums, "Mother Nature," p. 194.

51. Quoted in Guy McPherson, "Ellen DeGeneres," Comedy Couch, April 26, 2002. www.comedy-couch.com/interviews/edegeneres.htm.

52. Quoted in People Staff, "On with the Show," *People*, November 19, 2001. people.com/archive/on-with-the-show-vol-56-no-21/.

53. Quoted in Notable Biographies, "Ellen DeGeneres Biography."

54. Bret Fetzer, "Editorial Review of Ellen DeGeneres's Here and Now DVD," Amazon, accessed February 8, 2018. www.amazon.com/Ellen-DeGeneres-Here-Casandra-Ashe/dp/B0000CDRW5/ref=sr_1_1?ie=UTF8&s=dvd&qid=1243378812&sr=8-1.

55. "The Funny Thing Is …," *Publisher's Weekly*, accessed February 8, 2018. www.publishersweekly.com/0-7435-3361-5.

56. Quoted in Notable Biographies, "Ellen

DeGeneres Biography."

57. Quoted in Rome Neal, "Something's Fishy with Ellen," CBS, May 29, 2003. www.cbsnews.com/news/somethings-fishy-with-ellen/.

58. Quoted in Notable Biographies, "Ellen DeGeneres Biography."

59. Quoted in Phillips, "Catching Up with Ellen DeGeneres."

60. Quoted in "President Obama Names Recipients of the Presidential Medal of Freedom," Office of the Press Secretary, The White House, November 16, 2016. obamawhitehouse.archives.gov/the-press-office/2016/11/16/president-obama-names-recipients-presidential-medal-freedom.

61. "President Obama Names Recipients," The White House.

62. Quoted in Phillips, "Catching Up with Ellen DeGeneres."

63. Quoted in Lacy Rose, "The Booming Business of Ellen DeGeneres: From Broke and Banished to Daytime's Top Earner," *Hollywood Reporter*, August 22, 2012. www.hollywoodreporter.com/news/ellen-degeneres-show-oprah-winfrey-jay-leno-364373.

64. Quoted in Phillips, "Catching Up with Ellen DeGeneres."

65. Quoted in "Ellen DeGeneres Upset at Prop 8," *St. Petersburg Times*, November 7, 2008, p. 2B.

66. Quoted in Chloe-Lee Longhetti, "'We Like Uninterrupted Conversations and Furniture

Without Grape Juice on It': Ellen DeGeneres Says She and Wife Portia de Rossi Don't Regret Not Having Children," *Daily Mail*, June 4, 2016. www.dailymail.co.uk/tvshowbiz/article-3625612/ Ellen-DeGeneres-wife-Portia-Rossi-no-regrets-not-having-children.html.

67. Quoted in "A&E Greenlights New Docuseries 'Little Funny' from Executive Producer Ellen DeGeneres," A&E Networks, September 16, 2016. www. aenetworks.com/article/ae-greenlights-new-docuseries-little-funny-executive-producer-ellen-degeneres.

68. Quoted in Judith Newman, "Ellen Enchanted," *Ladies' Home Journal*, March 2009, p. 121.

69. Quoted in Mackenzie Schmidt, "Tour Ellen Degeneres' Incredible Homes, Past and Present," *People*, March 24, 2017. people.com/home/ellen-degeneres-houses-bought-sold/ellen-degeneres-the-anti-house-flipper.

70. Quoted in Phillips, "Catching Up with Ellen DeGeneres."

Ellen DeGeneres Year by Year

1958

Ellen DeGeneres is born on January 26 in Metairie, Louisiana, to Betty and Elliott DeGeneres.

1971

DeGeneres's parents separate.

1974

DeGeneres moves to Atlanta, Texas, with her mother and stepfather.

1976

DeGeneres graduates high school and moves back to the New Orleans area.

1978

DeGeneres reveals to her mother, Betty, that she is a lesbian.

1982

DeGeneres wins Showtime's Funniest Person in America contest.

1986

DeGeneres appears on *The Tonight Show* and becomes the only female comedian to be called over to talk to host Johnny Carson on her first appearance.

1989

DeGeneres appears in the sitcom *Open House*.

1991

DeGeneres is voted best female comedy-club stand-up performer at the American Comedy Awards.

1992

DeGeneres appears in the television show *Laurie Hill*.

1994

These Friends of Mine debuts and is renamed *Ellen* for the fall 1994 season.

1995

DeGeneres releases her first book of humorous essays, *My Point … and I Do Have One*.

1997

"The Puppy Episode" of *Ellen*, in which her character, Ellen Morgan, reveals she is gay, airs in April; DeGeneres appears on the cover of *TIME* magazine with the headline, "Yep, I'm Gay."

1998

Ellen is canceled.

2001

The Ellen Show premieres in September but is canceled after just one season. In November, DeGeneres hosts the Emmy Awards after the terrorist attacks of September 11.

2003

DeGeneres launches *The Ellen DeGeneres Show*; releases her second book of humorous essays, *The Funny Thing Is …*; and voices Dory in the Disney/Pixar movie *Finding Nemo*.

2008

DeGeneres marries Portia de Rossi on August 16.

2016

DeGeneres is awarded the Presidential Medal of Freedom by President Barack Obama.

2017

DeGeneres and de Rossi celebrate their ninth wedding anniversary; DeGeneres becomes the recipient of the most People's Choice Awards in history; *Ellen's Game of Games* premieres.

For More Information

Books

DeGeneres, Betty. *Love, Ellen: A Mother/Daughter Journey*. New York, NY: Rob Weisbach, 1999.
Ellen's mother—one of the people who knows her best—describes Ellen's early life and career from her point of view.

DeGeneres, Ellen. *My Point ... and I Do Have One*. New York, NY: Bantam, 1995.
This is DeGeneres's first book of humorous essays, which give readers some insight into her own life and her thoughts on life in general.

DeGeneres, Ellen. *The Funny Thing Is ...*. New York, NY: Simon & Schuster, 2003.
DeGeneres's second book offers even more humorous essays from her creative mind.

Shoup, Kate. *Ellen DeGeneres: Television Comedian and Gay Rights Activist*. New York, NY: Cavendish Square, 2017.
Although Ellen is famous for her comedy, she is also active in improving the lives of members of the LGBT+ community. This book covers her successful career and activism.

Websites

The Dian Fossey Gorilla Fund International
(gorillafund.org)

A cause that is close to DeGeneres's heart is animal rights, and one of her heroes was animal rights activist Dian Fossey. One of the gifts Portia de Rossi gave her wife for her 60th birthday was the foundation of the Ellen DeGeneres Campus of the Dian Fossey Gorilla Fund International.

The Ellen DeGeneres Show
(ellen.warnerbros.com/)

Visit this website to enter contests, write an email to DeGeneres, buy DeGeneres merchandise, or view segments from her popular daytime talk show.

The Ellen DeGeneres Wildlife Fund
(ellendegenereswildlifefund.org)

The second gift de Rossi gave DeGeneres for her 60th birthday was the foundation of the Ellen DeGeneres Wildlife Fund. As of early 2018, its only project is the partnership with the Dian Fossey Gorilla Fund International. Learn about the dangers facing mountain gorillas in Rwanda and what can be done for them.

Human Rights Watch: LGBT Rights
(www.hrw.org/topic/lgbt-rights)

As a champion of LGBT+ rights, DeGeneres has encouraged people to understand the discrimination this community still faces around the world and to get involved to stop it. This website has up-to-date news concerning the LGBT+ community.

Twitter: *The Ellen Show*
(twitter.com/TheEllenShow)

Follow DeGeneres on Twitter to read her posts and have a chance to win free tickets to her show.

Index

A

Abdul, Paula, 85–87
Abercrombie, Clyde, 39, 46
Advocate, 69
Allure (magazine), 40, 70
American Civil Liberties Union
  (ACLU), 62
American Idol, 85
Atlanta, Texas, 18–19, 24, 27, 96

B

Becker, Karen, 86
Beginning, The, 8, 71, 78
Ben, 20–21
Best Daytime Talk Show Host,
  79
Big Bang Theory, The, 76
Bill of Rights Award, 62
Birmingham, Alabama, 61
breast cancer, 40–41, 88

C

Carson, Johnny, 38, 47–49, 96
Chance, Greyson, 87
Christian Science, 10, 12–13,
  15, 17–18, 40
clean humor, 46
Clyde's Comedy Corner, 39, 41,
  46
"Come Out with Ellen" day, 61
CoverGirl, 9

D

Dateline NBC, 30, 46, 66, 79, 83
Daytime Emmy Awards, 79
DeGeneres, Betty, 10, 12, 15–18,
22–24, 27–28, 30–31, 34, 36,
40–41, 46, 49, 51, 55–56, 58,
60, 66, 96
DeGeneres, Elliott, 10, 12–13,
15, 17–18, 31, 33–34, 51, 96
DeGeneres, Vance, 10, 15,
17–18, 20–21, 51
Disney/Pixar, 76, 97
divorce, 16, 18, 51
Doctor Doolittle, 76

E

Edtv, 77
eleveneleven, 87
Ellen DeGeneres: Here and Now,
  73–74
Ellen DeGeneres Show, The, 6–7,
  70, 72, 74, 78–79, 82, 87, 97
Ellen Show, The, 71–72, 97
Ellerbee, Linda, 68
Emmy Awards, 6, 8, 55, 65,
  71–73, 79, 97
Entertainment Weekly
  Andrew Stanton on *Finding
    Nemo* role, 76
  on Emmy Award hosting, 72

F

Falwell, Jerry, 59
farewell tour, 53
Favorite TV Personality, 79
Favorite Voice from an Animated
  Movie, 77
"50 Funniest Women Alive," 79
Finding Dory, 9, 76–77
Finding Nemo, 9, 76–77, 89, 97

Fresno, California, 68
Funniest Person in America,
   43–44, 96
Funny Thing Is ..., The, 64,
   74–75, 97

G
GLAAD, 62
Goodbye Lover, 77
Guardian, The, 50

H
Halo, 86
Harrelson, Woody, 68
HBO, 8–9, 47, 51–52, 71,
   73–74, 77–78
Heche, Anne, 66–70
Hedison, Alexandra, 82–83
Hollywood Squares, 72
house flipper, 88
Hunt, Helen, 65, 68
Hurricane Harvey, 88

I
Iger, Robert, 68

J
Jack Benny Award, 62

K
Kat, 27–28, 37–39, 47
Kids' Choice Awards, 77–78

L
Laurie Hill, 52, 96
LGBT+, 7–8, 29–31, 41, 55–56,
   59–62, 65, 69
Little Funny, 87
Lohan, Lindsay, 74
*Love, Ellen: A Mother/Daughter
   Journey* (DeGeneres)

"B," 18
coming out, 28
Ellen as miracle, 12
move to apartment, 15
on *The Tonight Show*, 49, 51
Love Letter, The, 77

M
MacPherson, Guy, 71
Marines, 46
Martin, Steve, 43, 46
Metairie, Louisiana, 10, 18, 96
mockumentary, as part of last
   Ellen episode, 68
Moore, Demi, 60
Morgan, Ellen, 7, 52, 55–56,
   58–61, 65, 67, 97
Mr. Wrong, 76
My Point ... and I Do Have One
   (DeGeneres)
   on childhood, 10
   on Christian Science, 12
   on Funniest Person in America
      title, 44
   on high school science classes,
      17
   New York Times best seller, 64

N
New Orleans, Louisiana, 6,
   8–10, 17–20, 25–28, 32–34,
   39–41, 44, 96

O
One Night Stand, 52
Open House, 51–52, 96
Oprah, 66
Oscars, 6, 66, 79
Outstanding Lead Actress in a
   Comedy Series, 65
Outstanding Talk Show, 79

Outstanding Writing for a Comedy Series, 65

P
People for the Ethical Treatment of Animals (PETA), 86
People (magazine)
  on breakup with Heche, 69
  on Emmy Award hosting, 72
People's Choice Awards, 79–80, 88, 97
PetSmart, 86
Phillips, Stone, Ellen's interview with
  on achievements, 89
  on audience dances, 81
  on clean humor, 46
  on daytime talk show, 79
  on decision to come out, 66
  on hot-button issues, 83
  on telling mother about homosexuality, 30–31
"Power Players Who Shape Your TV Habits," 79
PrimeTime Live, 61–62
Proposition 8, 85
Publisher's Weekly, 74
"Puppy Episode," 58–61, 65, 68, 70, 97

R
Reaching Normal, 77
"Riff Raff Room," 81
de Rossi, Portia, 9, 83–86, 88, 97

S
San Francisco, California, 41–42, 44, 47
Saturday Night Live, 6, 20, 72
Sawyer, Diane, 61, 66, 68

September 11, 2001, 72–73, 97
Simpsons, The, 76
stand-up comedy, 6, 8, 16, 26–27, 33–35, 42, 44–46, 51–53, 69, 71, 73, 78, 87, 96
Stephen F. Kolzak Award, 62

T
tabloids, 56
These Friends of Mine, 52–53, 97
Thornton, Billy Bob, 60
TIME (magazine)
  coming out and, 65, 97
  on Jerry Falwell quote, 59
  "100 Most Influential People," 79
Tonight Show, The, 38, 47, 49, 51, 96
Tulane University, 32

U
University of New Orleans, 25, 34

V
Variety (magazine), 6
veterinarian, 13–14, 86

W
Washington State, 13
Will & Grace, 55, 72
Woman of the Year, 86

Y
Young Comedians All-Star Reunion, The, 47

WHEN GOD WALKED THE EARTH

RICK JOYNER

MorningStar Publications
A DIVISION OF MORNINGSTAR FELLOWSHIP CHURCH
375 Star Light Drive, Fort Mill, SC 29715
www.MorningStarMinistries.org

When God Walked the Earth
by Rick Joyner
Copyright © 2007

Distributed by MorningStar Publications, Inc.,
a division of MorningStar Fellowship Church,
375 Star Light Drive, Fort Mill, SC 29715
www.MorningStarMinistries.org

International Standard Book Number—1-59933-105-5; 978-1-59933-105-8

Cover Design: Kevin Lepp
Book Layout: Dana Zondory

Unless otherwise indicated, all Scripture quotations are taken from the
New American Standard Bible, copyright © 1960, 1962, 1963, 1968, 1971,
1973, 1974, 1977 by The Lockman Foundation. Italics in Scripture are for
emphasis only.

FOREWORD

When Napoleon read the Gospel of John near the end of his life, he reportedly said, "Either Jesus is the Son of God or the one who wrote this Gospel is! I know men, and no man could have made up a story like this." It is true, there has never been a story written or dreamed of like this one. It is simply beyond human genius to have conceived such a marvel and wonder as the Gospel of Jesus Christ. However, it is not a story. It is true, and it is actually the most verified account in history, with the evidence of it continuing to permeate the entire earth.

The Gospel is the account of the history of the greatest miracle of all—the majesty, wonder, and glory of God becoming a man and living among His own creation. God has done many great things throughout history to reveal Himself to His beloved creation, with the purpose of leading mankind and the earth back to reconciliation with Himself, but none can compare to the miracle of God coming and living among us.

5

The very concept that God Himself became a man and walked among us is so extraordinary and incredible that it is understandable that no one can really grasp it unless God helps them to. Only the Holy Spirit can open our eyes to the reality of this, regardless of the overwhelming evidence in history that this actually took place. We, therefore, should not fault the skeptics, but pray for them to have eyes to see.

We need to also pray that those who have seen and who have believed would have their eyes opened to see just how marvelous this miracle really is. How can anyone who has seen the love of God, which is manifested through Jesus, not be in perpetual awe and wonder at this love? How could anyone who really sees not constantly be on fire with a passion to make our glorious God known? There is only one way. For some reason, we closed our eyes to this greatest of all truths and started focusing more on this present world.

This book is not written for skeptics, but for believers. It is not written to convince you of the reality of this miracle, but to hopefully remind you of just what a wonder and marvel it is, and how wonderful our God is, which is forever proved by this greatest of all historic events. He emptied Himself and became one of us so that we might ascend from the depths of our depravity to become like Him. This is one of the ultimate questions: Are we still ascending?

The true Christian life is the greatest adventure and the highest quest that any human being can experience. Are we living it? Or have we lost our way and sunk back down to the temporary cares of the earthly? Even if you have lost your way and sunk back to the cares of the earthly, you can rise again and soar into the heavenly realm that is your true home.

As we proceed toward the end of this age, this bridge between the heavenly and natural realms will be found by more and more people, and the supernatural will become more and more natural to all who believe in Him. However, our goal is not to just live in the supernatural, but to live in Him.

This book is a portrayal of what it was like to behold this greatest of miracles—God becoming a man and walking among men, from both the human perspective and the angelic, which is the spiritual realm. This is not to add or subtract one thing from the biblical narrative, but to help us grasp the spiritual, supernatural perspective. This greatest of all miracles is the foundation of our faith and it is supernatural; the true Christian walk is supernatural.

This book began when I was going through a period of having extraordinary prophetic experiences almost every week. I was being caught up into another realm at times and seeing things from the spiritual perspective, including the great spiritual battles on earth. These experiences were very hard, often very frightening, but at the same time wonderful beyond description. I was shown many things about the future, and this was very exciting, but my greatest love has always been history, and the greatest history of all is the account of Jesus walking the earth. In one experience, which I wrote about in *The Final Quest*, I saw the crucifixion. It was almost more than I could take, and I was undone by this for weeks.

I love the Gospels, and read them over and over, all of them at least once a year, but no amount of reading had ever impacted me with the cross the way that experience did. I could not stop thinking of Mary, the mother of Jesus, the other women who followed Him, John, His beloved disciple, and the incredible courage they had to stand there and watch the One they loved be tortured. But even more than this: What was it like for the Father to watch this happen to His beloved Son? I only saw it in a vision and I could not endure it— how did they see the real crucifixion and endure it? It was because of love that they all endured it. It was because of love that Jesus endured it.

After my experience of beholding the cross, I never wanted to see it again, and at the same time I wanted to see it again more than anything. As I said, I love seeing things in the future, but I was drawn even more to seeing the past, especially the time when Jesus walked the earth. I have come to understand that the Lord somehow dwells beyond time, outside of time looking in, which is why He knows the future just as well as the past. I asked Him if He could catch me up in the Spirit and show me the past just like He had shown me future events before. He did. This book is some of what I have seen from that perspective.

This narrative does not add or take anything away from the biblical Gospels. I would not accept as truth anything that did. I realize that many of my books, such as *The Final Quest, The Call,* and *The Torch and the Sword,* have been hard to classify. Some put them in the prophetic section, and some in the fiction section. I am fine with either classification. It would have been much easier and probably made the books more palatable to many more people if I had just called them fiction, which many counseled me to do. However, I felt that this would be dishonest, and truth is the most valuable commodity we have.

I know that these are not fiction, but I also know they are not Scripture. They are from real experiences, and I tried to record them as accurately as I could, but we "see in part," and we **"see through a glass, darkly" (see I Corinthians 13:12 KJV).** I am also such a concept-oriented person that my memory for details is extremely weak. Even so, I was given the perspective that I share in this book for an important reason. The true Christian life is a supernatural life, which is basic because we are called to worship a supernatural God, and we must worship Him in spirit and truth. Like it or not, believe it or not, all who continue to pursue God through Jesus Christ will grow to be more at home in the spiritual realm than the natural, earthly realm.

Christ now dwells in unapproachable light and glory that is far more awesome than we can even comprehend or behold in these earthly bodies. He is no longer Jesus of Nazareth, but He is the Lord of glory above all rule, authority, dominion, and power. Even so, there is something about the life He lived on earth and the cross that He endured which will forever be the greatest revelation of His nature—who He is. The ultimate goal of seeing what He did is to relate to Him now, who He is and where He sits. When I was shown this natural and spiritual perspective, it helped me to do this. I believe that it can help you.

The "real world" is the spiritual realm, not the earthly. This realm is called but "a shadow" of the spiritual in the Scriptures, and that is indeed what it is. If we really believe the Bible, we do not just believe that all of the recorded events in it happened, though that is important, but we believe God to see the same things happen in our own lives. That is true faith in God and the Bible. Understandably this greatest of all events, God becoming a man and living among His own, was to compel us to live the way that He lived—in every way.

How can we live the way that Jesus lived? Of course, He lived a life of truth with a holy, single-minded devotion to doing His Father's will. We might translate "holy" as being "wholly" His. Jesus has given us the same Spirit by which He did His works. His Spirit will lead us to Him and convict us when we depart from Him. His Spirit will grow His character in our lives and give us the power to do the same works that He did. This one truth will keep us on the path of life and always lead us to victory—it is all about Jesus. It is seeing Him, knowing Him, following Him, becoming like Him, and doing the works that He did. That is our ultimate purpose in this life, and everything else that happens in our lives is meant to help bring this to pass.

If this book achieves its purpose, it will impart a greater devotion to pursue a deeper understanding of this greatest of all events—how God became a man and lived upon the earth, and how He is still becoming man and walking on the earth, through us. He still seeks to do the same works that He did when He walked the earth, through us. Before the end of this age, there will be a people who walk the earth just like Jesus did, doing the works that He did, and even greater works, because He now sits at the right hand of God and has sent His own Holy Spirit to be in those who follow Him.

The glory of God is about much more than just beautiful colors or heavenly music—it is about His nature. King David wrote that the Lord showed His acts to the children of Israel, but to Moses He revealed His ways (see Psalm 103:7). I make no apology for the fact that I love to see the works of God, especially miracles, but it is a far greater treasure to know His ways—why He does the works that He does. This is the highest quest of man—to know the Lord and His ways and to be in such unity with Him that He can use us to do His works.

As we get closer to the end of this age and the dawning of the age in which the Lord Himself will take His authority and rule over the earth, this bridge between the spiritual and natural realms will become an essential and vital truth for the very survival of Christians. We do not war against flesh and blood, but it is a spiritual battle against spiritual powers, and we must understand this if we are going to prevail in this battle. We have been given divinely powerful, spiritual weapons as Christians.

We are not alone in our journey to serve the Lord, or in this battle between light and darkness. We are actually in partnership with angelic majesties whose purpose is to minister to the heirs of salvation. The New Testament encourages us to understand angels, as well as to recognize them, and even at times show them hospitality, just as many of the Old Testament saints did. Showing hospitality to angels is not just to entertain them, but it is to further establish our partnership with them in the purposes of the Lord on this earth.

The Lord loves His angels too, and they love Him and us. They, too, have a great part in His plan, and though it is not our place at this time to be overly concerned about that, we do need to understand our partnership better. It is a part of building the bridge between the natural and heavenly realms. The building of this bridge was a basic purpose of Jesus, as He explained in John 1:48-51 when He first addressed Nathanael:

> Nathanael said to Him, "How do You know me?" Jesus answered and said to him, "Before Philip called you, when you were under the fig tree, I saw you."

> Nathanael answered Him, "Rabbi, You are the Son of God; You are the King of Israel."

> Jesus answered and said to him, "Because I said to you that I saw you under the fig tree, do you believe? You shall see greater things than these."

> And He said to him, "Truly, truly, I say to you, you shall see the heavens opened, and the angels of God ascending and descending on the Son of Man."

By this Jesus was declaring Himself to be "Jacob's ladder." Remember when Jacob was fleeing from his brother and he laid down to sleep and had a dream of a ladder reaching into heaven? The angels of God were ascending and descending upon it, and he saw the Lord at the top of the ladder. The Lord declared to Jacob the

same promise that He had given to Abraham and
Isaac. When Jacob woke up from this dream, this is
what he said:

> Then Jacob awoke from his sleep and said,
> "Surely the Lord is in this place, and I did
> not know it."
>
> And he was afraid and said, "How
> awesome is this place! This is none other
> than the house of God, and this is the gate
> of heaven" (Genesis 28:16-17).

Jacob declared here a truth about the house of
God that will become an increasing reality in these
times. The house of God is **"the gate of heaven."** The
house of God, the church, is called to be the gate of
heaven where the messengers of God ascend into the
heavenly realm and descend back to the earth with
evidence of heaven's reality. That is who Jesus was and
what He did His whole time on the earth, and that is
what He wants to do through His people now. As we are
told in Revelation 4:1:

> After these things I looked, and behold,
> a door standing open in heaven, and the first
> voice which I had heard, like the sound of a
> trumpet speaking with me, said, "Come up
> here, and I will show you what must take
> place after these things."

This door is still open. The Lord is still beckoning
us to come up to where He sits and sit with Him. The

true Christian life should lead to where we are more at home in the spiritual realm than we are in the natural realm. We should see more clearly with our spiritual eyes, the "eyes of our hearts," than we do with our natural eyes. True Christianity is supernatural because we are called to worship God who is Spirit, and those who worship Him must worship Him in spirit and in truth.

During times of great moves of God on the earth, the appearances of angels to humans inevitably increase. However, this is not as much because they are entering our realm as it is the result of people beginning to enter their realm—the spiritual realm. Being able to enter the spiritual realm should be as normal to Christians as entering their homes. This will become an increasing reality to Christians as we get closer to the end of this age, as the sure prophecy of Scripture declares in Acts 2:17-18, which is a quote from Joel 2:

> "And it shall come to pass in the last days," says God, "that I will pour out of My Spirit on all flesh; your sons and your daughters shall prophesy, your young men shall see visions, your old men shall dream dreams,
>
> "And on My menservants and on My maidservants I will pour out My Spirit in those days; and they shall prophesy" (NKJV).

The previous Scriptures tell us that "in the last days" these prophetic experiences, dreams, visions, and prophecy will be for the old and young, male and female. So as we get closer to the end of this age, we can expect these to increase, and they are increasing. This is one of the signs that we truly are in the last days.

We also see in this text that these prophetic experiences are the result of the Holy Spirit being poured out. Prophetic experiences are actually one of the surest signs of a true outpouring of the Holy Spirit. One of the results of being touched by the Holy Spirit is that He begins to open the eyes of our hearts, or our spiritual eyes, so that we begin to see into the spiritual realm. Those who are born again into the new creation will begin to see the kingdom of God. As the Lord explained before Pilate, His kingdom is not of this world, or this realm.

As the Apostle Paul later wrote to the Corinthians, he became more at home in the spiritual realm with the Lord than he was in his physical body. This is the nature of those who are maturing into a new creation. Elisha could sit on the side of a hill in perfect peace, even though a whole army was about to attack him because he could see into the realm of the spirit. We would not be overly concerned about any conditions on the earth if our spiritual eyes were truly open. If our spiritual eyes are open, we will see something even greater than Elisha, who saw myriads of angels protecting him— we will see Jesus, who sits above all rule, authority, and dominion.

If we truly see Jesus and where He sits, and we know that we have been sent by Him, how could we fear anything or anyone on this earth? The Lord Jesus Himself walked this way, seeing what the Father was doing, and He gave us His Holy Spirit so we could walk the same way. Being born again is just the beginning of our new creation life, just as being born is the beginning of our lives in the natural realm. Our spiritual nature is something we must grow up into, which is in truth, growing up into Christ, becoming a functioning member of His body on the earth.

We cannot see the kingdom without being born again, but not all who are born again see the kingdom. Many who are born again refuse to see for fear or other reasons, and they may mature somewhat, but will remain quite blind spiritually. This must change. The reason these prophetic experiences are being poured out by the Holy Spirit **"in the last days,"** is because we are going to need this kind of guidance through the times. We must have our eyes opened to see, and we must mature in our spiritual nature.

The way that Jesus preached the kingdom was to demonstrate its authority over any conditions on the earth. Jesus Himself was God touching the earth with heaven. In heaven, there are no cripples, so when Jesus touched a cripple on the earth with heaven, he was healed. There is no lack in heaven, so when the great need of more than five thousand hungry people with only one little boy's lunch to feed them arose, the Lord just gave that little lunch a touch from heaven, and it multiplied until all were fed and a lot was left over. In the time to come, when the last great trumpet of God is sounded, which is the preaching of the gospel of the kingdom, those who preach it will do so with the power to demonstrate the kingdom of heaven's authority over the earth and any conditions here that the Lord wants to touch with heaven.

When Peter got out of the boat and walked on water, he was not literally walking on the water, he was walking on the Lord's Word when He said, **"Come" (see Matthew 14:29).** The Word of the Lord has more substance than the firmament. If the King of heaven said to a mountain for it to be plucked up and cast into the sea, and we were used by Him to do this, the whole world would be astonished, but the angels in heaven would probably be bored. They have seen much greater things than this—they have seen Him stretch out the heavens like a tent curtain.

We do not have in human language terms that can describe just how awesome our God is. It is His gentleness with us that allows His kingdom to be declared by **"the foolishness of preaching" (see I Corinthians 1:21 KJV).** When the Jews asked Jesus for a sign from heaven, they wanted Him to do something in the sky, such as stop the sun like He did for Joshua, or something of that nature, which in no way could be done by a mere man. The Lord could have easily done this, but it was not the Father's time for that, so He did not. However, at the end of this age, we can expect much of that type of demonstration of heaven's authority over the earth, which is what the rest of the text in Acts 2:19-20 makes clear:

> **I will show wonders in heaven above and signs in the earth beneath: blood and fire and vapor of smoke.**

> **The sun shall be turned into darkness, and the moon into blood, before the coming of the great and awesome day of the Lord (NKJV).**

We are in the first stages of the time when the Lord will send messengers who will trump anything that even Hollywood has been able to imagine about men walking in supernatural power. I used to teach that many had moved mountains one shovelful at a time, but then the Lord chastised me in a dream for teaching that. He told me that those who had even a little faith could tell any mountain to be plucked up and cast into the sea, and it would obey them. He also said that this was going to literally be done before the end of this age as a witness that His Word is true.

There will be messengers released on the earth who walk in that kind of faith and of power because they see. They do not just see conditions as they are on the earth—they see the Lord and where He sits. They see what He wants to do and they are used by Him to do it just as Jesus was used by the Father to do His will.

My prayer for you is that this book will help you to have faith to begin to see, to have the eyes of your heart opened, and to begin to live the kind of supernatural life you have been called to live. Some are entering now. Many others will follow, and by them earth is about to be invaded again by heaven. If you are on this earth now and know Jesus, this is your calling. It is who you really are. As one of the ancients said, "We are not called to be human beings who have occasional spiritual experiences, but we are spiritual beings who have occasional human experiences."

This is true, and it is exciting, but let us never forget that it is all about Jesus. He is the Ladder. The rungs on the Ladder that extend into heaven are the progressive revelation of who He is and where He is. That Ladder goes both ways, touching heaven and earth, because He loves man and He loves the earth. He will restore both mankind and the earth from all that was caused by the Fall. He is redeeming, reconciling, and restoring. Above all, He is love. We cannot truly mature in Him without growing in love for Him and for all that He loves.

As we are told in the first chapter of the Gospel of John, which is the Gospel given to especially reveal

His heavenly nature, Jesus is both the Creator and the reason for the creation. As we are told in Ephesians 1:9-10, **"He made known to us the mystery of His will, according to His kind intention which He purposed in Him with a view to an administration suitable to the fulness of the times, that is, the summing up of all things in Christ, things in the heavens and things upon the earth...."** The highest purpose of man is to be found in Him.

Of course, there is far more to perceiving and understanding God than perceiving Him when He walked the earth. He is no longer Jesus of Nazareth, but He is the Lord of glory! He is resurrected, and He sits in more glory and power than we can fully perceive in this flesh. Our goal should be to see Him and relate to Him as He is now. However, we cannot get there without crossing the bridge of relating to Him when He was a man. Understanding Him then is the launching pad to perceiving Him in His present glorious and heavenly state. This book is an attempt to actually lift off that launching pad and begin to see in both realms. There is only one door through which we can safely do this, which is to see Him in all things.

When He walked the earth, few could recognize Him and even among those who did, few really understood Him. To recognize and understand Him as He still moves among us by His Spirit is the greatest challenge and greatest quest that we can pursue in this age. My prayer is that this will somehow be used to stir you to that ultimate quest as the chief focus and joy of your life. To know Him and do His will is the most noble cause.

What I am writing about here is what I saw with my own eyes—the eyes of my heart or my spiritual eyes. I saw it because I asked to see it. The Gospel of John also leaves us with one of the most compelling verses in the Bible, which is John 21:25, **"And there are also many other things that Jesus did, which if they were written one by one, I suppose that even the world itself could not contain the books that would be written"** (NKJV). I know there is a library in heaven that contains these books, which are called "the books of life." To me, one of the great joys of heaven will be access to these books. Even so, I do not think that it is profitable to speculate about all of the other things that Jesus did. What we have been given in the Gospels is what we need to know now. I was shown what was already written in the Gospels, but from the perspective of the spiritual realm. It does not add to the story in the Gospels, but simply gives another perspective of them. I am not sure this is necessary or even profitable for everyone, but it did help me greatly. Even so, before continuing I would like to add a caution.

As a student of history, I am well aware of the tragic damage done to the gospel and the church by the

Gnostic teachings and Gnostic gospels. I have been deeply provoked by the speculation, which led to exaggeration and a terrible distortion of the truth that originated from the Gnostic teachings. This drove me to search out and become totally convinced of the canon of Scripture and to be devoted to its integrity as the only source for the doctrine of the church. The prophetic gifts cannot take the place of the Scriptures and are not given for the establishing of doctrine. The Bible alone must be the only basis for establishing doctrine. This must never be compromised if we are going to remain on the path that leads to life.

I long to sit in that great library in heaven and read about all of the things that Jesus did when He walked the earth, or even better, to sit with Him and His disciples who were there, hearing them recounted. I was shown these events from the perspective of the spiritual realm, which stirred in me a much greater awe of what was taking place, and in some cases enabled me to understand them better—but it never added to the biblical account.

Sometimes what the Spirit reveals is so gentle that there can be a fine line between what you see prophetically and what you imagine. Every honest prophetic person will admit to this. The more you mature spiritually, the more you should be able to distinguish this line, but I do not yet consider myself so mature as to not occasionally, unknowingly, cross that line. I think what I have written here was a revelation, but I trust you to judge that.

Though this book may help to illuminate some things in the Gospels a bit, its real purpose is to stir an even greater love for the Scriptures, especially where the greatest depth of revelation in the Scriptures can be found—in the Gospels. All of the symbolism in the Tabernacle and its rituals, the outline of history in the seven days of creation, as well as in the account of the sons of Jacob and the tribes that emerged from them can be seen. We can grasp the meaning of the Melchizedek priesthood and the manifestation of the sons of God, but the greatest and deepest revelation of all is found in the life of Jesus when God walked the earth. Every event in the life of Jesus, every teaching, contains seemingly infinite layers of understanding that few ever begin to grasp. It is time that we understand them.

As we are told in I Corinthians, we see in part, know in part, and prophesy in part (see I Corinthians 13:9), even the greatest prophetic experience will only reveal to us a part of the whole revelation. This is why we have the four Gospels. Each has a part and reveals the Lord's walk upon the earth from a slightly different perspective. They do not conflict with each other, but complement and complete each other. That is why I like to read all four of them at least once a year.

Prophecy is often used for revealing the strategic will of the Lord or to help us keep on the path in this great adventure. From time to time, it is used to help illuminate Scripture, which is our map. One biblical example of how a prophetic experience can help illuminate Scripture is in the case of Peter's trance in which he saw the sheet lowered from heaven with all manner of creatures in it. It was the clear teaching of Scripture that the Lord would be a light to the Gentiles, but until that revelation came to Peter, it did not seem that the church had understood this.

Proverbs 4:18 declares, **"But the path of the righteous is like the light of dawn, that shines brighter and brighter until the full day."** The normal Christian life should be one of increasing light every day. True light is to see more of Him every day and thereby, to become more like Him and to be more used by Him to do His works. There are possibly infinite layers of understanding in the Scriptures and because of this, no story in it should ever grow old, but should be like the mine with the mother lode in it—there are veins of gold which lead to other veins, but the goal is to get to the mother lode, and the goal of our understanding is to get closer to God.

When Jesus was born on the earth, it was the most important event since the creation itself. It was a miracle so great and so marvelous that the angels who had witnessed His greatest wonders—even the creation itself—was so astonished by it that nothing before or since has so captured heaven's attention. That the Son of God would become a man and walk the earth in its tragic and corrupted state was beyond comprehension to even the highest angelic majesties. To understand it was the greatest quest in heaven. To those who see, to the wisest on the earth, it is likewise their greatest quest to understand.

As glorious as heaven was before this event, it was greatly illuminated by the wonder of this greatest miracle. Likewise, every life is illuminated to the degree that we comprehend this miracle. The more fully we can behold it, the more "the eyes of our hearts," or our spiritual eyes, will be open to see everything on the earth from heaven's perspective.

The coming of God to the earth will forever be the greatest demonstration of God's love and nature, and it will forever be the greatest beacon calling every soul to the safest of all harbors: reconciliation with God. God loves mankind so much that He has even chosen to make His dwelling place with us. When God was conceived as a man by the Holy Spirit, it marked the beginning of the "new creation," one even more marvelous than the first creation.

The conception by a virgin of the Son of God, who was born as a man to live and walk on the earth in its most corrupt and depraved state, and yet remain true to His divine nature, is not only the miracle which will forever trump all miracles, but it is the bridge between the earthly and heavenly realms. When anyone just begins to perceive this miracle, the conception of the Son of God by the Holy Spirit, he can be born again by the same Holy Spirit as a new creature, part of the new creation.

As has been well said, Christians are not earthly beings who are called to have occasional spiritual experiences, but we are spiritual beings who have occasional human experiences. As the Apostle Paul explained to the Corinthians, we should be more at home in the spiritual realm with the Lord than we are in the body (see II Corinthians 5:8). The "natural state" of the mature Christian is more spiritual than natural, but it is both. The new creation is intended to be the bridge between the heavenly and the earthly.

That God Himself would come to the earth at all, this tiny little speck of dust floating about in His great universe, was cause for marvel to the hosts of heaven. That He would send His Son to become a man, to redeem such pitiful little creatures who have so arrogantly rebelled against Him—that He would suffer humiliation to be concluded with the worst abuse and torture, all for the love of even those who were doing this to Him, is and will forever be the greatest revelation of God.

Forgive me if I keep repeating this, but it is a continuous echo in the hearts of all who pursue the truth. God came to us to compel us to seek Him. It seems that we will be able to ponder this event, culminated at the cross, for all of eternity and still not fathom the depth and richness of its revelation of God. However, to the degree that we can see it, we will have illumination and we will be able to see.

The ultimate purpose of man is to know God, to fellowship with Him, and to bring Him pleasure. A lifetime spent to bring Him just one second of joy would have been a life well spent. There is nothing in all of creation as interesting and compelling as the Creator Himself. As King David marveled in Psalm 8:3-4, **"When I consider Your heavens, the work of Your fingers, the moon and the stars, which You have ordained what is man that You even are mindful of him, and the son of man that You visit him?"** (NKJV) This is the second most important question, and therefore must also be a part of our ultimate quest for understanding—to know what man is that he would so capture the interest and heart of God.

In spite of all man's present problems and flaws, and to some degree because of them, man is certainly interesting. I have recently asked a number of physicians how much they think is really understood by modern medicine, just about man's body. The most that any of them has yet estimated has been 30 percent. With all of the millions and millions of hours of research, the body is still a great mystery.

When I have asked the supposed experts about how much the mind of man is presently understood, all they said was that not nearly as much is known about the mind of man as the body, with one admitting that he felt it was maybe 5 percent. If this is true about the mind and body of man, how much do we really understand about man's soul, his spirit? If this is true about man, how much do we really understand about God?

These numbers should not discourage us, but rather intrigue and inspire us. We should look forward to an eternity of learning. Even if we have only discovered 30 percent of the facts about man's body, that knowledge has been very profitable. Even if we only know 5 percent about man's mind, that knowledge has also been profitable. If this little bit learned has helped us this much, how much more will we be helped as we gain more knowledge? Obviously a great deal.

The Lord created the natural and spiritual universes to be ever expanding, and therefore, forever interesting. Who cannot love the creation, the animals, plants, and the earth itself, which is wonderfully and marvelously made? Mankind is even more interesting and wonderful. Even so, knowing God is the ultimate and most interesting quest and treasure. The primary reason we should study the creation is not just to know about it, or about ourselves, but to better understand the Creator who made it all.

Man has proven to be easily distracted from the River of Life by the little tributaries that feed it. Indeed, the tributaries, or isolated truths, are fascinating, and as we begin to search out one, we can find that it has almost infinite depth and wonder. Though it may take eternity to fathom the depths of the love of God revealed in the cross alone, we need to add to this the way the cross impacted each human being, with their own unique perspectives, problems, and needs. The truth of the cross and the atonement will forever be the same, but it becomes ultimately personal for every individual, and through it God begins a wonderfully unique and personal relationship with all who embrace Him through the cross.

It may take eternity to understand why the God who created the universe would look down upon such a speck of dust as the earth and care so deeply about us. Even right now you are on His heart. He cares about you, what you think, feel, and if you love Him. If you see Him, you will not be able to help but to love Him. If you love Him, you will be accomplishing the highest purpose anyone could ever have—bringing pleasure to Him. If we love Him, we will not be able to help but to love His people too, because we know the pleasure this brings to Him. I pray that somehow this helps you to accomplish the highest and greatest calling—to love God and love His people.

A ndrew forced himself to look directly into the piercing eyes of John the Baptist as he waited expectantly for the answer. He had never seen John this way before. John was the most intense man he had ever known, but now he seemed distracted mentally—he was very far away. Finally, Andrew asked him again.

"What happened at the river today?"

The Baptist turned away for a moment to collect his thoughts before looking back at his young disciple, and then he apologized,

"I'm sorry. What did you say?"

His disciples had never witnessed this type of courtesy in John before, and it made them even more uncomfortable. It had been an extraordinary day. Something both frightening and confusing had happened that morning, and now John seemed as if he were a different person. It almost seemed as if his great fire had been quenched. The great intensity had suddenly subsided and something else had taken its place. Now there was a softness, even a kindness, in John.

The Baptist had never been an intentionally mean person, but he was so intense that he continually trampled the feelings of everyone around him. Now he seemed to be almost sensitive, though very distracted. Even though he was distracted, it almost seemed that he had finally found peace.

"Who was that man that you baptized this morning?" Andrew continued, at the insistence of the other disciples. "And whose son is he? We heard a voice say that this was his son, but we did not see anyone where the voice came from. We could tell that you heard it, too. Who said it? We could not see anyone, and we have never heard a voice like that."

That morning, as was their custom, John preached to the people while his disciples were baptizing them. Then John stopped and began watching them. He suddenly jumped up and approached a man who had been patiently waiting in line. Because of the clamor of the people, many of whom were wailing under the weight of their sins, the disciples could not hear what John said to this man. Then, John personally baptized this one man, a thing which he rarely did anymore.

This had gotten the attention of his disciples. Then a strange voice, which seemed to come right out of the air, had called this man his son. Everyone seemed to hear it, and started looking around for who had spoken, but there was no one on the banks or hills above them. This created a mild stirring throughout the entire crowd. When they looked back at John, he was all alone. Then he just walked off without saying anything to anyone.

What had begun as a very good day for their work became charged with a strange feeling that came over everyone. John's preaching that morning had been particularly strong and had greatly moved the people to repentance. Then this happened, and John just left. Gradually the people began to leave too. It had been one of their biggest crowds yet, but they left in some confusion. This did not seem good and the disciples were concerned. When John had returned, he just did not seem like himself, which finally compelled his disciples to approach him and ask what this was all about.

Because the Baptist was such an aloof person, it took courage for even his closest disciples to question him. Even when they had been distraught by the way he offended some of the nobles and priests, they held their peace. But now they felt that something very strange had happened, and they had to have some answers. Finally, the Baptist began to focus on them and spoke, not with confusion, but with great joy in his voice.

"Friends, this was the day that I was born for. I saw the Lamb of God. He asked me to baptize Him. Now my job is done, and my time here will soon end. I have finished my course. Now He must increase, but I must decrease."

Though the Baptist obviously had great joy in this, these words hit his disciples like hammers. They hardly heard the part about the Lamb of God, or the momentous statement that this had been the day that John was "born for." What jolted them more than anything was hearing that his time was almost up, and that he was finished with what he had been given to do. It seemed as if everything was just beginning. All of Judea was coming out to hear him, and even many of the priests were now coming to be baptized. They had the attention of the entire nation. How could they stop now?

John gazed around at each of his disciples with what almost looked like compassion, and continued,

"Friends, truly the kingdom is at hand. Please listen to me. The King Himself stood right in our midst today. He was the One I baptized when you heard the voice of God."

"The voice of God!" several exclaimed together. "Was that the voice of God that we heard?"

"It was. That was the Father saying, 'This is My beloved Son, with whom I am well

pleased.' Today I baptized the Son of God. He
is the One who existed from the beginning. Now
He is walking among us. These are the days of
the great wonders of God. He has come to us
Himself, in His Son. He walks among us as a
Man. He has come in humility like a lamb, but
I tell you, He is the great King, and He is a
Lion! He will set up a kingdom that has no
end. This is the One that I was sent to prepare
the way for. He was here today!"

John paused as if he would drift back into the
faraway state he had been in for so many hours.
Andrew quickly begged him to continue, asking him
again about the voice.

"That voice was the Father. Even so, many
of you are going to witness even more glorious
things in the time to come. The One about
whom the angel spoke is now taking His
place among us. My time is up, but His is just
beginning. I leave fulfilled because I have seen
Him. I saw the heavens opened and the Holy
Spirit descended . . . and He remained on Him.
He is the One who will baptize you with the
Holy Spirit and with fire!"

Then the Baptist stood up and walked off by
himself. His disciples knew that he was going to pray
and that he would talk no more until the next day. They

watched him until he was out of sight. Then they began talking among themselves.

"What does all of this mean?" one of them asked, looking at Andrew.

"All along John said that he was just pre- paring the way for another," Andrew replied. "He did say that the One he was waiting for was much greater than he. I thought that he was talking about the Messiah—but the Son of God! God walking among us as a Man! But we all heard the voice, and there was no one around who could have spoken that way. This is hard to understand. Maybe tomorrow he will tell us more."

"But what does it mean that John's time is up?" asked another, without even trying to hide his emotions. "We have been through so much together. We have stood by him through every- thing. He has probably offended every power- ful person in the country now, and we are known to be his disciples. What will we do if he leaves? Where would he go? Where will we go? We know that he is a prophet sent from God. We cannot just give up everything that we have risked so much to build. In spite of the rage of so many of the leaders, the whole nation is listening to us now."

For the first time, John the son of Zebedee, spoke up with a deep but controlled passion.

"Have you not heard what the Baptist said? He said the Son of God was right here today! And we all heard the voice. It had to be God— no one else was near to where the voice came from. We have all known great times with the Baptist. Our hearts have been plowed, but in a way that gave us hope. The nation is stirred because God is speaking to His people again. We have been the most privileged to be this close to him. But it seems that something even more wonderful is now here. We must not look back, but forward. The prophet said that the Son of God was here today. I intend to find Him tomorrow."

The faces of some betrayed their skepticism, but John continued,

"I love the Baptist. I love him more than my own father. He is our father in many ways. I am so thankful to have been able to be so close to a real prophet sent from God. But if this is the Son of God, He must also be the Messiah. If He is, we must now follow Him. The Baptist himself said that his time was up, but the time of this One who is the Son of God is just beginning."

Except for Andrew, the others just could not consider leaving the Baptist. They had too much invested in him and his message. The group began to break up. In just a few hours, they had gone from feeling ready to take over the nation to having serious doubts. Feelings of an impending end of something wonderful started to come over them like a fog coming in from the sea. But for John and Andrew, a new and greater hope was just awakening.

This little band of John's disciples composed mostly of common folk, had risen to the pinnacle of spiritual influence throughout Judea, a place of influence they had never dreamed that they could have; they simply were not ready for it to end. Their hopes and dreams in the Baptist had grown every time they heard him preach about the coming kingdom. Now they could even picture themselves with important positions in that kingdom. They just could not give that up so quickly.

They also had grown to respect the Baptist more than any other man. Never had they known anyone so free from the fear of man, so confident, and so focused on his mission. The power of his vision and resolve swept up even the most learned and powerful into a new and living hope in the God of Israel.

The disciples who were with him day after day had also witnessed such a harmony in unfolding events that it was apparent that the very hand of God ruled his every move. Their days were filled with awe and wonder. These disciples just could not joyfully embrace the possibility that something so wonderful, and so obviously ordained by God, could come to an end so soon.

John and Andrew had never been very close to each other, but they had both become very close to the Baptist. Now, as they were obviously both thinking similar things about the events of the day, they turned to each other to talk.

"What are you thinking my brother?" Andrew began.

"Could this possibly be the very Son of God? If so, this is the most important day of our lives, and nothing should keep us from finding and following Him."

"I have been thinking the same thing. But how can we find Him? Do you think John knows where He is? Do you think that we can even approach Him? John said that He had come in humility like a lamb. There is something burning in me now to get to know Him. Even John said that this was what we had been doing everything for, to prepare for the One who was coming. Once He has come, can we go on preparing for Him? Isn't it time to follow Him?"

"Yes. I feel the same way. We must ask John to help us find Him. If there is One who is so great that even John said that he was unworthy to untie His sandals, how can we not follow Him? Maybe He will even let us serve Him like we have the Baptist. What greater thing could a man do than to serve the Messiah?"

"No doubt that would be the greatest thing we could ever do. However, our dear friends here all seem to just feel lost and discouraged. Being with the Baptist has been more wonderful than anything that I ever dreamed I would be able to experience in my life. This has been like living the Scriptures of old. Even so, if what John is saying is true, we must go on to find this One whom we have been preparing the way for. I do not want to be presumptuous, but how can we rest if One who is even greater than John is close by, much less the very Son of God Himself? We must find Him and try to become His disciples or His servants. Is this not what John trained us for?"

"We will have to ask the Baptist about all of this as soon as he returns from prayer. I know that I will not be able to sleep until we know more about this man. To think that we may have seen the Messiah today! But I must admit, it is hard to actually think that He is the Son of

God and that He existed before as John said. We have seen marvelous things though, which can only be explained as being from God. I do not believe that John would overstate who this is that we have been trying to prepare the way for.

The angels who were guarding the encampment listened intently. They all felt like the two disciples. They badly wanted to understand the events that they had witnessed that day. The Holy One Himself had come to this little band. Heaven had opened and the Holy Spirit descended like they had never seen Him do before. Now the heavenly realms were stirred like they had never before witnessed. All of heaven and hell seemed to be mobilizing.

Then a great angelic warrior appeared in their midst. They all lifted up their swords at once, and bowed low to salute him. The campfires all around suddenly blew with the wind stirred by his arrival. The great angel turned and bowed a salute to John's disciples, who were now shifting their cloaks to cover themselves from the wind this great angel's presence had stirred. The great angel then turned to the commander of the company of angels who surrounded their camp.

"Tell me," he asked of the commander, "How did these do today?"

"They know of the Holy One," the commander replied, "but they do not understand Him. They are actually discouraged by what happened today, except for those two over there."

"Yes, I know of them," the great warrior replied. "They will follow the Holy One. They are heirs. Because of their calling they will soon become known to the evil one, too. Therefore, two who are of greater rank than I will come to guard them. They will post their own warriors and messengers so that you will be relieved of their care. There are many others who will also be coming to take their positions with some of these people. The time has finally come. The battle is about to begin. You have done very well to keep them, but it is now time for you to be relieved."

"Sir," the commander of the band interjected, "if I have done well, can I remain with you, or be assigned to one of those who will join these disciples? Since we entered here, we have been in many battles, but the wonder of this is greater than anything we have known. We just cannot bear to think of leaving now. What we are seeing take place here is making all of the battles we have been through seem worth it."

The great angel's gaze intently surveyed this company of warriors.

"Your request will be considered. You are a good and faithful commander and will do well in the battles ahead. However, now there are some things of great importance that I must inform you about that will be hard for you and your warriors to understand."

"Please tell me, sir," the commander entreated.

"The evil one is intent on just one thing now—destroying the Holy One and His elect. Since he was foiled with his scheme to use Herod to do this, he has been in a great rage. Very soon the dark one himself will appear to tempt the Holy One. We have been instructed to let him do it. If he is not able to tempt the Holy One to follow him, he will be so enraged that he will try to kill the Baptist. You must let him do it."

"What?" gasped the commander.

"Yes. You must let the evil one kill the Baptist."

"Why? Even the great ones say that the Baptist has been one of the most faithful men that we have ever been given charge over. We were all sure that he would be taken up in the chariot like the prophet Elijah or even be translated like Enoch. Sir, please forgive me, but I must be sure about these orders."

"Yes, you heard me correctly. And I understand what you are thinking. But do not fear. This is a victory for him and for us. Today the Baptist finished his course. He has done everything that he was given to do. Of all the prophets, he has been the greatest! Even so, the elect are here now. The Baptist was the greatest of servants, but these are the heirs. The Baptist is as faithful as any man has yet been to his calling, but even he will not understand what is about to take place. He is from a different time and a different covenant than they are."

"But your excellency! I do not mean to question orders, but must we let the evil one kill him? Can he not be taken with more honor than that?"

"I do not understand all of these things myself. But I have watched many prophets and righteous men killed by the evil one. His power of darkness is great, but it is limited. Every time he uses his power to kill a righteous one he is weakened for a time, and it allows many others to behold the light of truth. In fact, I have been told by those above me that many of the heirs are to be killed by him also."

"Your excellency! This is very hard to accept. Could we possibly stand by while he kills the heirs? This does not seem possible!"

"I'm sure that we will be told more if we need to understand more. The Father's ways on this earth are a great mystery. Things are very different here. He only assures us that in the end we will all understand. We have been told that it is because the heirs will love the truth more than they love their lives, and that their willingness to die at the hands of the evil one will work to so weaken him that in the end, even one of your company will be able to bind him."

"Sir, I am a veteran of many battles, and though I know that what you are saying must be true, it is still very hard to comprehend. I, too, have seen it weaken demons when they wound or kill a righteous one. In fact, I have witnessed that the more light one has who suffers their attacks, the more it does weaken the evil ones who attack them. But are the heirs not called to retake this world from the evil one and rule over it with the Son?"

"That is correct," the great warrior angel responded. "But somehow they will retake this world by their sufferings. In this way, they will prove their devotion to our God, and it will so weaken the evil one to be able to attack those with such great light, that in the end, even the lowest of the angelic ranks will subdue him. He will expend himself in wrath against them.

"There will be many righteous ones who are allowed to suffer this way, and they will walk in far more light than we have yet seen in men. The willingness of these holy ones to suffer at the hands of the evil one will be what utterly defeats him. We have been given this knowledge because the time will come when many of us will have to let those whom we have been given the charge to protect fall into the hands of the dark ones."

"I just cannot understand how the Holy One could allow this to happen," the commander wondered aloud. "We know that He is here like a man to take back what Adam lost. How is it that He will allow the evil one to continue killing His own righteous ones after He has retaken authority over the world? Why would He then allow His fellow heirs to fall before the evil one? Why will He then not allow us to fight the evil hordes? The battle would be great, but we could easily defeat them, and these would not have to suffer."

"This is still a great mystery," the mighty messenger continued. "The ways of the Father are far beyond our ability to understand at times, but we do know that they are always wise and righteous. We were told that the heirs are to have this 'honor' of dying for the truth. By this they are proving their faithfulness, not to Him, but to us. It is true that whenever a prophet or righteous man has suffered for not compromising the truth, I have been filled with awe and respect for them. I have also witnessed even the great commanders of the evil one not being able to restrain their own respect for them when they do this, as much as they might try to hide it. It is a marvel."

They stood together looking over the little band of men with obvious wonder and affection. Then, the great angel continued, speaking loudly enough for the whole band of warriors to hear:

"Those who are so weak and confused for most of their lives can also love the truth and the Holy One more than they love their lives. When you see this you will begin to understand how some of them may even rise to become heirs with the Holy One. As difficult as it is to understand many things that take place here, the courage and faithfulness of those who are weak, who will stand and resist the evil one himself, is one of the great marvels we have been honored to behold. The entire host of heaven envies our commission to be here.

Even those assigned to the far galaxies spend most of their time inquiring about the things that we have been chosen to see here."

"You are right, sir," replied the commander, saluting his superior who was obviously about to leave. "I would not trade my place here for even the highest order of authority anywhere else. Thank you for this great trust."

"You would not be here if you had not earned it with your own faithfulness. I will pass on your request to stay."

As the great warrior departed, all of the angelic soldiers raised their swords in a salute. They had been allowed to hear what their commander had been told. They had already increased their vigilance watching over the disciples, knowing that some of them were the elect. Now, because they had heard that the evil one would himself come to test the Holy One, they were far more alert.

The heavens were now so stirred that there was an almost continuous passing of both angelic and demonic messengers. Angels of great power would at times light up the entire sky with their brilliance. Great winds, and even storms, were stirred up on the earth as they passed.

"The mobilization has begun," the commander said to his company.

The spectacle grew until his soldiers soon forgot about their own recent visit from such a great warrior. At the same time the disciples began to seek shelter from the wind and impending storms. The company of angels followed them closely.

Suddenly, two great angelic captains with their thousands appeared before the little company guarding the disciples of the Baptist. They stepped up to the commander who bowed low before them. The company of warrior angels all raised their swords high while bowing to one knee. The captains acknowledged their salute with a nod and then asked the commander to stand.

"We have come to assume responsibility for two of these disciples, John and Andrew," one of them said.

"They are the ones still talking over there. They have not slept, and the light of the Spirit of Truth has been upon them," the commander replied.

As the captains turned to see them, they drew their swords and bowed low to the ground as the entire host that was with them did the same. The commander and his company stood by awkwardly.

When the captains arose, they turned back to the commander and said, "Well done, Commander. We relieve you of your duty to these two. Over the next few years many of the other disciples will also be commissioned, and then other captains will come for them."

"I understand," replied the commander.

Then the two angelic captains turned to John the Baptist, who was now standing nearby, looking at John and Andrew.

"The Holy Spirit has told him about these two, and tomorrow he will direct them to follow the Holy One. These will be the first; their destiny is great. The mystery of God is about to be revealed. Permission has been granted for you to stay on the earth, but for now you must stay with the Baptist and the other disciples until relieved and given another assignment."

"Thank you, sir. Please thank the captain of our host for me."

"You can thank him yourself. You will see him soon."

"Michael is coming here?"

"No. He has been here for many years. He is cloaked with humility like his Master," said one of the captains.

"He's the messenger who stays with the Holy One!" the commander exclaimed. "We had no idea that he was our captain!"

"Yes. That is him. You did not know him because he did not want you to. He did not want to draw any attention to the Holy One, and it was not yet time."

"He is very well cloaked. I actually talked with him today and had no idea."

"You will see him again tomorrow. He will trust you with other important matters because you have been found trustworthy, and you will need to know them for your future assignment."

"Do you know my future assignment?" the commander inquired.

"I know something about it. You will help a man who is now a young Pharisee. He is one of the elect and will one day be as resolute as the Baptist. I do not know anything else about him, but I know that if you are being assigned to him, he is a man with a great mission. You are now a renown warrior among the hosts. Those who you are assigned to will be those with a great mission."

John and Andrew did not sleep at all that night. It was as if they perceived the stirring in the heavens that was taking place all around them. Both had determined that they would do all that they could to find the One whom the Baptist had called "the Son of God."

The next morning the disciples talked very little as they ate their bread. Crowds were already forming to hear the Baptist. None of them wanted to believe John's words, that his time was now up, and they were all hoping that the new day would bring the old John back. Then he appeared, as usual, about an hour after dawn.

The Baptist did not go down to the bank and begin preaching as he usually did. He just sat on a rock and looked over the crowds without saying anything. Then he called John and Andrew and told them to stand beside him. He did not say anything to them for nearly ten minutes. Finally, just as both disciples were about to unleash a barrage of questions, the Baptist stood to his feet, looking intently at a man who was walking alone by the bank.

"That's Him," the Baptist almost whispered. "Behold, the Lamb of God who takes away the sins of the world."

John and Andrew both began to breathe heavily. Their hearts were leaping within them.

"Is that the man that you called 'the Son of God?'" John almost demanded as he studied Him.

"He is the One. Do what is in your heart to do," the Baptist continued, motioning for them to go.

The two disciples then did something they had never done before—they embraced the Baptist. His faint smile let them know that it was all right, maybe even appreciated. Then he nodded again toward the One he had called the Lamb.

Having seen the strange sight of the two disciples embracing John the Baptist, the others gathered around him to ask what was happening.

"Where are those two going?"

"It is time for them to follow another," the Baptist answered.

The hearts of the disciples fell when they heard this. They had been such a tight group having been through so much together. With all of the confusion from the day before, it was hard to see anyone leave their company. Even so, none of them spoke because they were surprised by the obvious joy that was on the face of the Baptist. Seldom had they seen him even smile, but now he was smiling broadly.

John the Baptist discerned their thoughts and answered them just as if they had been thinking out loud.

"He is the Bridegroom. I am the friend of the Bridegroom. My joy is made complete just by seeing His joy. I have baptized you with water, but He is the One who will baptize you with the Holy Spirit and with fire! He is the One I came to prepare the way for. He is the One whom all of the prophets came to prepare the way for. He existed from the beginning. Now He will take away the sins of the world."

They all stood and watched as Andrew and John approached Him. They were only a few paces behind Him, but did not seem to know what to do next. Then He turned and looked at them. The two disciples almost fell backwards. Their hearts were beating so hard that neither was able to say anything.

"What do you seek?" He asked.

Finally, John spoke up, "Rabbi, where do You dwell?"

Jesus smiled. "Come and you will see," He replied, motioning for them to join Him.

John and Andrew were beside themselves with joy and relief. They both wanted to ask Him a thousand questions, but they were determined to use discretion. Again John spoke up.

"We are disciples of the Baptist. He told us some things about You. Do You mind if we ask You some questions?"

"Please, be free," He answered.

His tone was so calm, even friendly, that the disciples actually began to feel comfortable enough to freely talk with Him. Andrew then spoke up.

"Rabbi, we heard a voice yesterday when You were being baptized. We could not figure out who it came from. Last night the Baptist said that it was the voice of God...."

Jesus stopped and looked each of them in the eyes. The Baptist had penetrating eyes, but His were even more so. They felt completely exposed as He gazed at them. For a moment they felt very uncomfortable. He then reached out and put a hand on each of their shoulders to calm them.

"There are many things that I must tell you, but they would be hard for you to bear right now. John was sent to prepare the way before Me and he has done well. He has also prepared you well. There are some things that I will tell you, and there are some that you must receive directly from My Father. You will hear His voice again many times, both from within your own hearts, and without as you did yesterday, but the greatest is to hear from within. I know you heard His voice, and I know you believe. Do not be afraid. To follow Me your eyes and ears must be opened to things that you cannot now understand, but I will prepare you for them."

The Baptist and his disciples were still watching as the three passed over the hill and out of sight. John somehow knew that it was the last time he would see Him. Even so, he was not sad. He wanted to follow Him too, but had already been told that he could not. He was the last messenger of a Covenant, and Jesus alone could be the Bridge between the Old and the New that was coming.

The Baptist had been told that he would soon join those of his order, all of those who had prepared the way for this day. How he longed to meet them! He longed to be a part of the great cloud of witnesses who had earned the right to watch all that was about to unfold on the earth. He also longed to see the Father and the great hosts of angels who attended Him, a few of whom he had briefly met in this life.

Now that John's task had been completed, he began to earnestly long for death to the earthly realm so that he could live fully in heaven. Even so, he was a servant. He determined to serve each day with all of his heart until his time came to depart. He looked at his disciples. He knew that many of them would one day follow the Lamb. He had to do all that he could to prepare them for it.

The Baptist then turned and descended the hill to the bank of the Jordan, reciting the commandments of the Law with brief illustrations of how each was being broken by the people. He then recited the judgments that were promised for those who transgressed. He knew that they would never know they needed a Savior if they did not know God's righteousness, what He expected of His people, and how terribly they had all failed Him. A great resolve came over him to make this even more clear in the short time that he had left, and to prepare those who had been entrusted to him for the great events to come.

With a voice that reached even the fringes of the multitude, his words cascaded down upon the people like waves from the sea. Soon men were openly weeping and women were begging for mercy. His disciples took heart. Now, if possible, it seemed that he had even more fire than before. From that day John had an even greater reason for his work. He had seen the King, and he had seen the heavens opened. The kingdom of heaven had come to earth and was now walking among them.

Jesus shared His dwelling that night with John and Andrew. Encouraged that He seemed to genuinely enjoy their company, they talked to Him far into the night. He patiently listened to them and answered their questions. By the time they laid down to sleep, they felt as if they had known Him for a long time. They had. One day they would realize that they had known Him from the beginning. He was the One who stirred their hearts whenever the Scriptures were read. He was also

the One who touched them with joy when they
beheld the beauty of a sunset, or appreciated the grace
and dignity of a righteous man or woman. All things
had been made by Him and for Him, and in Him they
were all held together. He is the Word of God, the
communication from the Father to His creation, and
the ultimate desire of that creation.

As tired as John was from not sleeping the night
before, he had trouble sleeping again. As he looked at
Jesus across the room, he just could not believe his good
fortune. He was now sure this was the Messiah. He was
the coming King of Israel! He was the true King, not
like Herod. Would He have mighty men to serve Him
like David? Could they be some of these mighty men?
Would they do exploits for Him like David's men had
done for him?

Would He be an even greater warrior than David?
Yet, He was more patient, and even more humble,
than anyone he had ever met. John shivered from the
sense of the glories that he was about to behold. These
were the days that the prophets had all spoken about,
and he, John the son of Zebedee, was privileged to be
in the very center of them.

Andrew also laid awake for a long time with his
thoughts. He pondered some of the answers that Jesus
had given them to their questions. He seldom answered
their questions directly; He rather seemed to know what
they really wanted to ask but did not know how. He

listened to their hearts, rather than their words. Andrew then thought of his family, and Simon, his brother. Jesus had told him and John that they needed to return to their families, and that He would find them later. He said that He had to go into the wilderness for a time, alone, but He promised to come again for them. Though Andrew did not want to leave Him so soon after meeting Him, he could hardly wait to tell his family about the One they had found, especially Simon.

The two captains stood at the door of the little cottage. Their legions of angels were arrayed about them. Messenger angels were constantly passing by, but each would stop to salute the men in the cottage. The heavens were now opened. They now knew that the very fullness of the power of God dwelt in a Man. The One who spoke the universe into being now walked upon the dust of the earth. None of them had even dreamed that they would see such things when they were assigned to this tiny little planet! How could such a humble place even get the attention of the King like this?

When the Son had left His place on the throne, all of the hosts of heaven marveled. When He entered the womb of the young girl, they were astonished. Angels watched over each star. Great ones watched over many stars, and the greatest ones even watched over galaxies. But there was not one angel in the universe who would not trade his entire dominion to watch over a single man on earth. Men had taken on a whole new importance. They had now become the center of the universe.

"We have been on the earth since we were first assigned to guard the Tree of Life in the Garden," one of the captains said. "Now *that* Life walks as a Man. If any man knew who this was sleeping here...."

"Yes, but even the two here with Him do not really know. I have watched men for four thousand years now, since we drove the first two from the Garden. They have grown steadily in evil, just like the evil one. Their hearts and minds are continually set on evil. They have continued falling since the Garden, deeper and deeper into darkness. Now, even when they do good to one another, it is for selfish reasons. This has not happened anywhere else in the creation. I wonder constantly why the Father does not just destroy this little pocket of darkness. Instead, He sends His own Son! Even a speck of dust from this realm should not be allowed near Him; yet there He is, one of them!"

"The darkness in the hearts of men is becoming greater," replied the other captain.

"After being here for so long it is hard to understand how they will ever be brought back to the light. But here is the Light Himself, and we know nothing is impossible for Him. But how is He going to do it?"

The two captains bowed low to the ground as Michael stepped beside them. He was clothed as a messenger angel, but the captains recognized him.

"I have been listening to you," Michael said, beckoning them to stand upright. "I understand very well what you think about this race of men. All of the evil in the universe has been concentrated here on this little speck of the creation, this planet, and in these little creatures. Yet, there is a reason why the evil one has concentrated all of his power here. There is a destiny on man that is greater than any that man has ever comprehended, or even those of us who have been here from the beginning have comprehended. The Father Himself intends to dwell here among them, in the fullness of His glory. Men will one day be the eternal dwelling place of God."

The two captains both gasped with astonishment at this statement.

"For the Son to come here was more than I have been able to understand," replied one of the captains, "but for the Father to choose to dwell with them here, in His glory?!"

"Yes. There is a great capacity in men to do evil, but this is because there is also a capacity for them to rise to the greatest heights of nobility and courage. They will be able to think, feel, and love the way the Father does."

"I have seen nobility in some men for brief periods," one of the captains said thoughtfully. "Enoch, Abraham, Moses, David, and a few others grew so great in the light that they almost overcame the evil in their hearts. But there have been less than one in a million who even cared to know the God who made them. How will this entire race ever be made capable of seeing His glory, much less being His dwelling place?"

"It is beyond my ability to understand as well," Michael admitted. "I just know that the Son is here to completely recover the earth. He will return it to the condition that we knew in the Garden. I was even instructed to now call Him 'the Son of Man,' instead of 'the Son of God.' He has come as the last Adam to recover all that the first Adam lost."

They both then fell silent for a time as they gazed at their King, sleeping. They looked at the other two who had been chosen to see His glory and be His messengers. No angel in heaven was as foolish and weak as they were, yet here was the King sleeping beside them. Michael then continued.

"The first Adam walked where there was only good, but turned to evil. This One will walk where there is only evil, but will only do good. He will reveal the light of life to men, and they will begin to come out of the darkness. There will only be a few at first, but as the darkness continues to grow in mankind, so will the light. Many will follow Him back to the love of the Father. These are the elect. In time, the elect will prevail, and many will be saved from the darkness because of them. One day, because of these who are now so weak and foolish, the whole creation will forever know the strength of truth, that the light is greater than the darkness."

"If the light can prevail here, no one in any realm of heaven will ever question that," one of the captains agreed. "Even the darkest evil lords cannot get much more evil than we now see here."

"I wish that were so. It will get darker," Michael replied. "The fall is not yet complete, and it must be allowed to run its full course. Just as the Son has now manifested Himself in man, so will the evil one do the same. The evil seed that he sowed in man will fully mature in time. Then the earth will be even darker than this. But the light that the Son has brought to His own will overcome it. The light in even one of His little ones is greater than all of the darkness of the evil one. It is hard to understand all of this now, but I have seen the prophecies given to men as an oath from God, so it is sure.

"I am telling you captains this now, because it will appear at times like the light has been defeated. You must never despair, regardless of how it appears to go here. The greatest courage is always revealed when it appears that defeat is inevitable. There are many mysteries that we cannot now understand, but we will later. Only remember that the Father has Himself given His word to men that it will be so, that truth will prevail. For this reason we can be sure."

Andrew awoke first. It took him a minute to get his bearings in the unfamiliar surroundings. Then he saw John and remembered Jesus with a start. Quickly looking around the little cottage, and not seeing Him, he shook John to wake him.

"Wake up, John. Where is He? Did you see Him leave?"

John quickly sat up, wiping his eyes. Then the events of the previous days came cascading down upon his still sleepy mind. Glancing around the tiny cottage, John almost shouted:

"Where is He? Did you see Him leave?"

"That's what I just asked you!" Andrew shot back. "Let's go find Him."

Quickly gathering, putting on their sandals, and wrapping themselves in their simple shawls, they started to bolt through the door just as Jesus opened it.

"Good morning," He said, glancing at them. "You seem to have slept well."

Backing up to let Him in, John was the first to reply, "We were just going to look for You," and then added after an awkward pause, "I trust that You also slept well. I hope that we did not bother You too much with all of our questions last night."

"No. You will never bother Me with too many questions. I enjoyed them. Here, I have brought you some bread," Jesus said, handing each of them a loaf.

"Sir, You should have sent us out to get bread," Andrew mumbled, embarrassed to think that he had slept while the Messiah Himself had gone out to get bread for them.

Jesus seemed to just disregard Andrew's remark, and continued. "After we eat, I must go to be alone for a few weeks, and you must return to your homes."

Stunned, John quickly interjected, "Master, we have followed the Baptist for many months, and now we want to follow You. Please do not make us leave You."

Jesus looked up at them and asked patiently, "Do you not miss your families?"

John and Andrew looked at each other, and then John answered, "Yes. We do miss them, but there are sacrifices that one must make to do the will of God."

"This is true," the Lord responded, "but not all sacrifices are His will."

John and Andrew both pondered this for a moment before John spoke up again.

"After being with the Baptist we will never be satisfied with normal lives again. And now that we know who You are, how can we return to our families? We love them, but we could never return to the lives we had before."

Beckoning them to sit, Jesus continued, "Understand that I must go away alone for a time, but I will return for you. Until I do, please enjoy your families. You will make many sacrifices to follow Me, but I have come to sacrifice for the sake of families. You must enjoy yours when you can."

Andrew and John were visibly relieved. They knew that when He said He would return for them it meant that they were accepted as His followers. They both watched Him as He sat and began giving thanks for their bread.

As the three sat talking, the captains who watched over them listened to every word. They were still amazed at how casual these two men were with the Son and how casual He was with them. The stars sang His praise, with an uncountable host of angels at His bidding, yet on this little speck of dust called "earth," no one recognized Him or honored Him. Even more amazing was that He seemed to *enjoy* being on such a casual basis with people. This was something they had never seen or even considered in heaven.

As a messenger angel approached them, the two captains turned to receive him. To their astonishment, it was Gabriel himself. They both bowed low on one knee and saluted with their swords, as did the thousands of warriors arrayed about them.

"Greetings. I have come with your orders. Each of you is to keep your warriors and remain with these two men. They will be parting from the Lord for a time, and you must watch over them. Michael will himself stay with our Lord."

"It will be done. We will watch the two. Michael talked with us last night and we assumed that he would remain with the Lord."

The captains still had the look of astonishment on their faces as they watched Gabriel, so he continued,

"I know you are wondering why I came. It is true that I do not come unless there is the beginning of a new age, and that is why I am here now. A new age will begin on the earth."

"Sir," the other captain replied, "you just came to speak to the virgin, so why are you back so soon? Is another age beginning already? It does not seem that this one is yet complete."

"True," Gabriel replied. "When the Son came to earth it was the beginning of a new age. Even so, another age for man began two days ago. The Son will not be here much longer, but the age which just began will last as long as the earth."

All of the angels in the area were keenly listening as Gabriel spoke, and he looked about to be sure that they would all know that he was speaking to them, too.

"When the Son went down to the prophet John to be baptized, you saw the Holy Spirit come to Him and remain upon Him. He came as a dove, as a symbol of the dove that Noah released from the ark, which did not return to Noah. Man could not find his rest until the Holy Spirit returned to rest in man. The Son is the first man that the Holy Spirit has been able to descend upon and remain. There will be others whom the Spirit will be able to remain with, many of whom are now being born. When the Spirit can rest upon men, men will then begin to find their rest in God. This is the beginning of the final stage of the restoration of man to God."

"This is unfathomable!" one of the captains replied, as the entire company of angels who were standing by shifted noticeably.

"Yes. The Son has become a man to begin preparing men who can receive the Holy Spirit."

"Sir," the captain continued in a tone of protest, "we heard the message given to the Baptist—that he was to prepare the way for the One who would baptize with the Holy Spirit, but how can He remain upon men, other than the Son?"

"Good captain, I understand your question, but I am afraid that even I do not fully understand the answer. I do know that when the Son accomplishes His work here, men will begin to change. Many will become vessels within whom the Holy Spirit will be able to abide. Men will become the dwelling place of God. Looking at them now, it is very hard to understand, but they were created for this. God will restore them to their ultimate purpose."

"I have seen how the Holy Spirit loves men and loves being with them, even though they are so contrary to His nature," one of the captains interjected. "Even though He is holy and they are so wicked, He always seems to be looking for an opportunity to draw close to them and to help them. Watching Him has helped me to love both men and God even more. I for one am very happy for men, even if it is beyond my understanding of how this will ever be."

"We are all learning a lot about our God as we learn about men," Gabriel replied. "The virgin, who carried the Son, brought such joy to the Holy Spirit and has been such a delight to the Son since He has been here. Even if it is a great mystery to us, it is wonderful to see their joy in men. There is such darkness and evil here; it is a marvel when any of them turn to the light. Those who do become a special delight to God."

"You understand much," Jesus replied, as if He had been involved in the entire conversation. Gabriel, the captains, and the entire host knelt, bowed their heads, and drew their swords in a salute that caused the entire mountainside to glisten with a fiery glory.

Michael was standing with Him as He gazed over the host, and then toward John and Andrew who were just beginning to walk down the narrow road. As Michael nodded toward the two, the host began falling in behind them. Other companies of hundreds began taking positions over them or in front of them. The procession was more magnificent than any that Caesar had ever beheld, yet John and Andrew were completely unaware of it.

"These did not choose Me, but My Father chose them, even before the foundation of this world," Jesus explained to Gabriel and the captains. "They are two of the elect. They are My brothers. Treat them as you would Me."

"Thank You for this great honor of serving Your brethren," the first captain replied as the other nodded his agreement.

"I know you will do well," Jesus replied as He began to walk down the road in the opposite direction of the two.

Suddenly, the mountains themselves seemed to disappear in a great flash of light as Michael drew his sword. Instantly, a great host of mighty warrior angels appeared, all of which seemed equal to the captains in power. Their swords were drawn and the fierce glory that emanated from them was a spectacle not often witnessed beyond the inner sanctuary of heaven itself.

The captains who followed Andrew and John were briefly stunned before instinctively drawing their own swords. Angels throughout the realm, in all of the little towns and villages, drew their swords and stood as if ready for battle.

"I had no idea there were so many of us here," one of the captains exclaimed to his companion.

"Nor did I," said the other. "But why the alarm…?"

As his words tapered off they both knew the reason. A terrible cloud was coming from the direction of the sea. This could be none other than the entourage of the evil one himself. As the cloud grew closer, great storms arose and began to thrash the coastal villages.

"Why does he delight in tormenting men like that? Look at him sending lightning to hit those little shacks and kicking up waves to turn over their boats. I would that the Lord would turn us loose on him. The power of Michael's sword alone could destroy him, and we could easily dispense with his entire host," the captain shouted as the evil clamor grew.

"He can flaunt the authority that he has now over the earth, but the time will soon come when we will be allowed to fight," the other captain reminded him. "But I believe he knows he cannot intimidate us. He simply hates men and delights in smiting them like that because he knows they think that God is doing it. He tries to make them think that God hates them so that they will not seek Him or want to be close to Him."

The angels in the villages now had their hands full guarding their new charges from the host of demons being released among them. There were many clashes, but the demons quickly learned not to touch the elect. Enraged, they charged off after men and women who were not protected. Terrible fights broke out in a multitude of homes. Demons of lust jumped on men, women, and children, causing more than a few to stumble that night. Insanity and fear attached themselves to others, aided by the atmosphere created with the storm. It was the beginning of a most unholy night in the land called "holy."

Michael drew next to Jesus as He walked. "Master, can we do nothing?"

"My heart breaks, too, good friend. I know that you have watched over My people of Israel for many centuries and have witnessed many terrible onslaughts of the enemy without being able to respond. The day will come when you can, but this is not that time. When we gave man the freedom in the Garden to obey or disobey, we gave them the freedom to choose their own master. I am here to give them another chance to choose, and the choice will be much more clear now that they have known the consequences of disobedience. But before I can help them, I must choose to walk in obedience as a man. Then I will be able to show them the way out of this terrible darkness. Even then not all will choose Me. Even so, if just a few return to My Father, it will be worth what I am here to do, because He loves them so much, as do I."

"But why has the evil one left Rome to come here?" Michael inquired.

"He has come to tempt Me just as he did the first Adam," the Lord replied.

"My Lord, I know You can dispense with him at will. How can he tempt You like that?"

"When I face him, it will not be as the Son of God, but as the Son of Man. I must do what the first Adam did not do. I must remain faithful. My Father gave this world to man to rule over it, and a man must take it back by obeying. I am that Man. That is why I came, and why I must face him as a Man, and not as God."

"I understand," the archangel replied. "I have understood that for a long time, but it is still so hard for us to restrain ourselves when we could dispense with him and his evil host so easily."

"I did not come to win back the world with power, but with love," Jesus continued. "Those who resort to power first will misuse their power. Love does not exist for power, but power exists for love. Not understanding this is what caused the evil one to fall. What I am doing here is not just for man, but for the whole creation. For all of eternity, the creation will study what is done and what I do here. It will keep many others from falling as Lucifer did."

"It was hard for all of us to watch him rebel the way that he did, and then to see You let him go forth to recruit for his rebellion without stopping him," Michael admitted. "It was a very confusing time for us all, but we have known Your goodness and the Father's goodness, and You are worthy of all trust."

Jesus stopped for a minute, and looked the great angel in the eyes. "The love of power will always lead to a fall. Only when we use power for love's sake will we use it rightly. I am not here to reveal power, but love. You know how easy it would be for Me to stop the sun like I did for Joshua, or even part the Great Sea, but this would so overwhelm men that they would choose Me out of fear whether they wanted to serve Me or not. I will only use power to reveal the power of My love for them. I do not want men to choose Me because of power, but because they love Me and love the truth. I will not be known as Power, but as Truth and Love."

"Master, Your ways are marvelous beyond our comprehension. All of the angels in heaven are growing in wisdom as we behold Your ways and deeds here," the great angel replied, his eyes glistening with emotion like a man's. "You have entrusted me with great power and great authority, but I have learned to value the honor of beholding Your ways even more than I do the power You gave to me. I treasure being able to feel love as I do now. Watching You causes me to grow in love, too. I can now say that I want to fight for these men because I love them, not just because I despise the enemy. I still do want to respond with power at times."

"You are wise, My friend," Jesus replied. "You were all brought forth with a purpose, and the power that has been given to you will be fully used. But you must always remember, for it to be rightly used, you must use it in love. Even when you are released to fight and destroy the evil ones, you must do it for the right reasons, which you are learning here. But now you must wait here and let Me go on alone."

The archangel stopped, but with obvious protest in his eyes. "Master...."

"It must be this way," the Lord replied. "I must go into this desert alone. You and your host must wait here."

Jesus walked on into the desert under a cloud of darkness such as had never been witnessed on the earth before. Demons of every kind were swarming through the mid-heavens all around and above the wilderness. The presence of the evil one himself was felt by the angels throughout the region, though he was not seen because of the great swarming darkness around him. No angel for a thousand miles would sheath his sword for the next forty days.

Several captains drew close to Michael, bowed, and saluted. For a few minutes he did not even seem to notice them, but then he beckoned them to come forward.

"Sir, what shall we do?" one of them asked.

"Stand at the ready, guard your charges, but do not attack," Michael replied, still looking in the direction in which Jesus had disappeared.

"Never have we seen the enemy gather like this," one of the other captains replied.

"You are new here, aren't you?" the archangel asked, turning to look at the captain who spoke.

"Yes sir. I have come from a far galaxy. I was sent here to watch over one of the elect who was just born today. I am thankful to get this commission, but it is already a little more exciting than I was expecting. Is this the beginning of the last battle?"

"None of us knows the time of the last battle, but what I do know makes me think that it may yet be many seasons from now. The elect whom you have been sent to watch will be mighty champions. They will prevail over the evil one. They will fight with a power that is greater than we angels possess; yet now most are still infants, and many are even yet to be born."

"How can that be?" several of the captains responded in unison with obvious surprise. "Why, they do not have even as much power as the least of the messenger angels. In fact, they do not seem to have much power even in their own realm—some are insignificant even when compared to the beasts," one of them continued.

"They will be given the power of the Holy Spirit," Michael responded. "When the Holy Spirit comes to abide in them, they will have more power than all of us together. The power that created us, and the heavens themselves, will be in even the least of them."

A great hush fell over the entire group of captains, which now numbered in the hundreds. This was incomprehensible to them—some were even tempted to think that Michael had somehow lost his reasoning, that this great darkness was affecting him. Finally, one ventured another question.

"How can the Holy Spirit abide in these who are so unholy? I have only been here a short time, and I have seen more evil in these men than I knew existed before. Even in the best of them, there is much evil! It is hard for me to understand how the Holy Spirit even touched the prophets as briefly as He did, to give them words and visions, but to abide in *these*?"

"I understand your questions, but I also know that the Son is here to make men holy again. Those who will be able to see His glory will be changed by it. Those who can see His love will be purified by it. There is a power in

His love that we have a hard time understanding, but these men will understand it. They will love Him with a great love because He will deliver them from so much. The great love that is about to be revealed by Him is itself a greater power than any power we have known before. It is so great that the time will come when we will all marvel more at the love He reveals here than we did over the power we saw released to create the heavens."

There was a long silence as the host of captains pondered this. Finally, one of them spoke. "Why did the Son walk into that desert alone? And why does the evil one and his host not flee before Him? They know who He is even though He has taken this form as a man."

"It is a marvel. If He lifted His finger, they would all flee. But He said that He must face the evil one as a man. He will not violate His own decrees. This world was given to man to rule, and man gave himself to the evil one. The Son has come as a man to win back this world, which He will do with His obedience. But even then He will not force men to return to Him. If He uses His power alone to turn men back to Him, He said that there would still be disobedience in their hearts. Then they could never become true worshipers.

"The time will come when He will use His power, and we will be allowed to use ours, but first He wants to gather those who love truth more than power. These are the heirs. Those who come because of His power will become subjects, but they will not be joint heirs like those who come because they love Him and love His truth. These are the ones who will be trusted with the power of the Holy Spirit, a power that is much greater than ours. They will be that trustworthy."

"His ways are more marvelous than we have ever comprehended," offered one of the captains.

"Yes," Michael replied. "When man chose to disobey in the Garden, and the wickedness of their hearts grew so deep as it did in the days of Noah, how badly we all wanted to destroy this little planet, along with the evil one and his hosts. We just could not understand why the Lord was so patient with these little creatures. Now we are seeing a glory in His ways that is so wonderful that even we are constantly being changed and matured, and we are loving God more than ever. Whatever He does that may cause us to doubt the most at first, as we are patient and watch, becomes an even more wonderful wisdom. These are both terrible and wonderful times."

John walked into his home for the first time in many months. The servants came running, calling to his mother that he had returned. Joy filled the house and was heard at the dock where James and his father were working on one of their boats. They knew what the commotion was about even before the servant reached them with the news. Smiling to each other, they arose and began walking to the house.

John flung his arms around his father while reaching over to knock his brother's hat off of his head. A good natured wrestling match was about to begin until Zebedee restrained them.

"Son, we have missed you more than you can imagine. We have all missed you. It is a great joy to have you back."

"I'm sorry, Father. I did not mean to be gone so long. But such wonderful things have been happening that I simply could not leave. I have so much to tell you. These are the times that our people have been waiting so many centuries for."

"Son, we want to hear all about it. But first, you must wash and change your clothes. We are going to have a feast to celebrate your return."

"Thank you, Father," John replied, hugging his mother again. "It is so good to be back here with you."

Giving his brother a big shove, John departed for his room, determined to wash and return as quickly as he could. Joy was flooding his soul. He felt as if he were the most blessed man alive. To have such a family, to have had the experience of being taught by John the Baptist, and then finding the Messiah! He was bursting to tell every detail to his family, but he knew the rules of the house. Dinner was the time for such conversation, which is why theirs usually lasted several hours.

It had been quiet for a few minutes. Finally Zebedee spoke up. "You're sure this Man is the Messiah? We have heard so much about the Baptist, and I was sure when I heard him myself that he was a prophet. I am so thankful that he would accept you as a disciple, but you know so little about this other Man. Are you sure that you heard the Baptist right? Is the 'Lamb of God' the same as the Messiah?"

James had said nothing, but was watching his brother's every expression. To him too, it seemed that John may have been a little too hasty to leave the extraordinary opportunity of being one of the disciples of the Baptist, knowing so little about this other Man.

"Sir," John answered, carefully looking at his father, "I know that you think I may have been hasty to leave the Baptist, but if you had been there, if you had heard the voice that we heard, and then heard what the Baptist said about Him . . . He said that his whole life had been a preparation for that one day. He said that now Jesus would increase and he would begin to decrease."

As the family reclined at dinner, all of the servants had come to sit around the room and listen. Zebedee was a considerate man, and he wanted them to all enjoy the celebration of John's return.

"Son," Zebedee continued, "I have watched you on a quest to know God from the time you were very small. I, too, have tried to serve Him all of my life. My greatest joy has been to see my sons become so devoted to Him. He has been very good to me, and I know that He will be good to you. I am sure that He will lead you in His ways. But after so many centuries, to believe that the Messiah could really be here; it just seems too wonderful to contemplate."

Finally, James spoke up. "Good brother, I know you well enough to believe that this Jesus is at least another prophet, and maybe even one greater than John. But for Him to be the Lamb, I just am not sure what that means, and I am surely not ready to say that He is the Messiah. But I must confess that John's testimony of Him must be seriously considered. I also know that John often said that he was preparing the way for the Messiah. Maybe they are the same, the Lamb and the Messiah. You're sure that this Man said that He would come for you in a few weeks?"

"That is what He said. But I am embarrassed to say, in the intensity of the moment, I neglected to tell Him where I lived. However, He knew that I had a family and that I needed to return to spend some time with you, and I am sure that I did not tell Him anything about you, so maybe He also knows where we live."

"If He is a prophet, I guess He will find you," James offered, with a snicker.

"I sure hope so," John replied, a little nervously.

"Well, I think that it is time to retire," Zebedee said, rising. "Those storms a couple of nights ago did a lot of damage. It will take us weeks to repair some of the boats and nets. And we were fortunate compared to some of our neighbors. I've never seen such fierce storms come up so quickly. It was as if the wrath of God was being unleashed upon us. I'm sure we deserve it. There must have been a dozen adulteries exposed in the nation last year, and now what Herod is doing is just too much to contemplate. These are dark times. There seems to be an unending assault on family. Family life is one of the greatest joys we have, and yet some seem intent on destroying it. It is madness!"

"Father, why would God judge us so severely when the rest of the nations are so much worse?" James half asked and half stated. "That does not seem right to me."

"Because we are God's chosen people. We must live by a different standard. He has given us more truth so He expects us to be different," Zebedee retorted, a little forcefully as if they had had the same conversation before.

John listened carefully, pondering every comment deeply. He resolved to ask Jesus about this. The way He had answered all of their questions the night they stayed with Him still amazed him. He saw everything from a perspective that was far above anything he had heard from the teachers of the Law. Certainly He would know the answer to James' question. The very thought thrilled John. The Baptist had once called Jesus "the Son of God." To think of being taught about God by God! That was too much for John to even fathom.

Simon was trying to be patient with his brother. He was very glad to see him, but he was also quite agitated that he had been gone for so long, leaving their fishing business when he was needed the most. Now with their only boat having been sunk in the storm, Andrew did not even seem to care.

"I'm happy for you to have found the Messiah, but I think we had better think about trying to find where our next meal is going to come from," Simon finally blurted out.

Andrew was a little stunned, and then he looked around at the mess that was still left over from the storm. "Of course. Please forgive me, my brother. I have not even asked you how things have been going. I heard about the storm and the boat as I came into town. You have a wife and family to think about. I can understand why you are worried. I'll be here for a while and will help get things going again."

"You mean you will be leaving again?" Simon asked, furrowing his brow in what Andrew knew was his most irritated gesture.

"Simon, I must. How can I not follow the Messiah? We, as a people, have lived for this time."

Simon spun around to look out over the sea. They both stood in silence for a few minutes, and then Simon spoke. "You're right, my brother. I know that we have spent centuries as a people waiting for Him, but I would just like to hear about one person who gets a prayer answered! I have tried my whole life to be obedient. I go to the synagogue every Sabbath, and I work hard for my family. Why does God then do this to us? Does He take pleasure in our torment? Life is hard even without such disasters."

Andrew knew better than to try to answer these questions. Finally, he stepped over to his brother, wrapped an arm around his shoulders, and pulled him toward the house.

"Come, I must see your wife and children. How I have missed them all! Everything will work out. It always does. Nothing will hold you down for long. It will just give the fish a chance to get a little bigger before we catch them."

"It is good to see you, brother," Simon said, finally smiling. "Only, I do not like to hear about you leaving again."

"I know. But we will have plenty of time to talk about it. The Rabbi will not be coming for me for several weeks."

"What? He's coming here?"

"Yes. He said that He would come for me in a few weeks."

"Very good. I would like to meet the Messiah," Simon retorted with a chuckle. "Do you think He can help us raise our boat, or better yet, tell us where the fish are?"

"Good brother, that may be a little too much, even for the Messiah. I think you're asking for something that only God can do."

Michael, the angelic captains, and their hosts continued gazing at the terrible spectacle before them. The wilderness had been overshadowed by the cloud of demons for almost forty days, since the Son had entered His confrontation with Lucifer. It had not been since the rebellion in heaven that two hosts faced each other like this. For forty days the evil horde of demons hurled insults and feigned attacks at the angelic host, who the demons knew were under strict orders not to respond.

These insults and feigned attacks were easier to endure than watching helplessly as the evil horde assaulted the population of Israel. They gathered into storms to send hail to destroy their crops. They mercilessly blew trees over into dwellings and struck people with lightning as if it were a great game to them. They afflicted men, women, and children with every kind of disease. They even agitated the Roman troops to mischief and sowed bitterness and rebellion in every heart in which they found an opening.

Michael understood this was an attempt to make it as hard as possible for Jesus' message to reach Israel. It would be hard for those who suffered such catastrophes to hear a message from God.

Through all of the temptations and mischief of the evil horde, Satan had but one goal—to get the Son to respond in His authority as God. The demons did not understand it, but their master, Lucifer himself, had said that they were doomed if Jesus did not abandon His manhood and respond to them in His power as God. They had to provoke Him to do something that the Father had not sent Him to do.

Lucifer himself looked down upon the spectacle. With his legions darkening the sky, he was feeling more and more confident. He looked at the angelic hosts standing passively and felt nothing but contempt. He turned to his lieutenants, waving his hand across the horizon where the angelic host stood, saying,

"They will soon be ours! Their Master will serve me, and then they will serve us. This is the moment that we have been waiting for! This is even better than when I seduced Adam and Eve—much better! How foolish for the Father to deliver the Son into my hands like this! He even sent Him in the form of Man, the weakest of all creatures at resisting me! You will soon witness my greatest triumph. We will celebrate by destroying this despicable little people, the Jews, which He, for some inexplicable reason, cares so much about."

Jesus sat on the hillside looking out over the wilderness. He longed for fellowship with His Father again. He knew that the Father was beholding Him, and He knew that the Holy Spirit was with Him, but He longed to behold the Father, and to feel the Holy Spirit again. Now He felt so weak. For the first time in weeks, hunger was coming upon Him in waves, and the cold seemed to grip the very marrow of His bones. This body of flesh had become more of a burden than He had ever known before. How He longed to be free of it!

He began looking at the rocks. They almost looked like bread. How easy it would be to turn one of them into a loaf and satisfy this terrible pain! Quickly, He caught Himself turning away from the rocks to look out over the countryside.

Then depression swept over Him like the waves of hunger had before. How dreary this world was! How He longed to see the Father's glory again. How tired He was of seeing the continual selfishness in the hearts of men! Everyone only sought their own good and cared only for themselves. If He were a King now, He could show them the evil of their ways! But wasn't that what so many other kings had tried to do, only to be reduced to an even more terrible selfishness? Then He would be no different from them. How could anyone ever rule such a stiff-necked people? With sudden awareness, He stood up and looked around. Where were these thoughts coming from?

"I must not continue to let My mind drift like this," He thought to Himself. "I am not here at this time to rule. I'm here to love them."

Then the weariness came over Him yet again, causing Him to jump up with a start.

"I'm the Son of God," He thought. "I not only dwell in the glory, I have the glory within Me. I have the power. I could even move the mountains if I wished. I could dispel this dreary weather with the lifting of My finger."

Lucifer saw his chance. The weakness of Jesus' flesh had now made Him vulnerable. He was tottering on the edge. Now He could be pressed into using His power for His own selfish reasons.

"And He thought that He would condemn me for using the power for myself and seeking glory for myself. He is about to show that He is

just like me!" Satan whispered to his commanders as he left them.

As Satan lifted up, the evil horde stopped swirling
and almost in unison gasped with a confusing combi-
nation of both ecstasy and fear. Wind swept across
the mountains so that the rain was driven before the
horde in sheets. Satan turned and thrust his hand in the
air as if directing his legions to back off. He despised
these whining little creatures and demons almost as
much as they feared him, but they were useful to him.
He directed his commanders to control them so that
they would again form a cloud of depression over
the area. He then proceeded toward the Son, almost
cheerful with anticipation.

Jesus had again knelt to pray, mostly to battle the
thoughts that were now seemingly bombarding Him
through the rain itself. Sensing the presence behind Him,
He turned and looked up at Lucifer.

Lucifer stood in his most glorious apparel—more
stunning than any earthly king could have ever imagined. His face was so kind and appealing, any child would
have easily come to him. Jesus knew him immediately
and slowly stood to His feet to face him.

"I am very sorry to see You like this,"
Lucifer offered, giving a slight bow. "We have
had our differences, but this is quite shocking.
You are, after all, the Son of God, and even the

One who created me. Is there something that I can do for You?"

They stared at each other for a long minute. Satan continued, "Of course, You, being the Son, do not need for me to do anything for You. I will be glad to turn the stones into bread for You, but I'm sure You can still do that much, even as weak as You are now."

Jesus looked at Lucifer. He looked more regal than the angelic captains. His face was more kindly than he had ever seen on a man. His voice was more soothing and compelling than He had heard since coming to earth. This was the voice that Eve had heard. He watched as Lucifer picked up a stone that in fact looked just like a loaf of bread.

"Dear Jesus. That is what You want me to call You now, isn't it? Please, turn this into bread. You deserve this after all You have been through. Your body needs its strength. Then we can talk. Of course, I will be glad to do it for You if You can't."

For a moment Jesus thought He could smell the bread. Never had He thought that anything on this earth could be so appealing. He took it out of Lucifer's hand. He held it, looked at it, and surprisingly, smelled the bread again, faintly, and it aroused His hunger like He had never experienced before.

"I have never desired bread like this before," Jesus admitted. "But My Father made this into a stone, and He has not shown Me that I am to turn it into bread. He loves Me more than the birds of the air, and He feeds them every day. So if He has not chosen to feed Me today, it is for My good, because He loves Me. I only want to eat what My Father provides for Me. Man does not live by bread alone, but by every word that proceeds from the mouth of God," Jesus responded, looking up at Lucifer.

"Of course," the devil responded, not changing his demeanor, or showing anything but his seeming concern. "So, the Father has stripped You of Your powers as well. Why would He do that if He trusted You?"

Instantly, Jesus and the devil were standing on the pinnacle of the temple.

"Listen, I am only doing this to help You," Satan offered, compassionately. "It looks like the Father has betrayed You just like He did me. If You are still His Son, if He has not disowned You, which it sure seems that He has done, cast Yourself off of this temple and see if He rescues You."

Jesus looked down, feeling faint from the lack of food. He wanted to jump just to feel the Father's love for Him again. He knew the Father would save Him, and it would be so wonderful to feel Him again! Satan continued.

"Do the Scriptures not say, 'He will put His angels in charge of You, to lift You up lest You dash Your foot against a stone?' (see Matthew 4:6) Surely then, He would send His angels to catch You if You were to jump off of this temple. That is, if He still considers You His Son. If He doesn't, You will know that He has done all of this to You just to destroy You. Then You will know that You are being cast away just as I was. I know that You do not want to use Your power for Yourself, but if He does not send His angels to save You, then You had better learn to use it for Yourself, just like I did. This is as good a time as any to find out."

Weakness was now sweeping over Jesus in waves. The hunger was becoming unbearable, and His mind clouded. Never had he felt this depressed. How He longed to see the Father or feel the Holy Spirit. How great it would be to just see an angel. He looked at the temple where He had enjoyed sweet fellowship with the Father whenever He had been able to visit it. He remembered conversing about the Scriptures with the elders when He was young, and what a delight it was to learn them, ponder them, and see them from man's perspective.

"No! I will not test the Father the way men are constantly doing it," Jesus finally replied. "To doubt His faithfulness is to doubt the power that upholds the universe which gave life to men and angels. This was the doubt that Eve allowed to take root in her soul. You, old serpent, you have not changed your ways have you? As the Scriptures declare, 'You shall not test the Lord your God,'" Jesus responded.

"Very well. I understand," Lucifer offered, in his most humble and compassionate voice. "It is just hard for me to understand why You are in such a state. But You are right. You know that You are the Son and You do not need to prove that.

"I must apologize for these uncontrollable demon hordes," Lucifer remarked as he turned to look at the chaos they were creating. "They are perpetually hungry, almost as much as You are. They must feed their appetites or they really get out of control. Since the curse upon us is that we must eat the dust, which You used to make the flesh of man, our only food here is the flesh of men. We therefore must satisfy ourselves with man's passions. The more we can inflame them, the more we ourselves are filled. Of course, men invite us to do that by turning from the words that proceed from the mouth of God and seeking their fulfillment through the lusts of the flesh. So we are feeding each other. But it is a pitiful existence for both of us," Lucifer said, turning to look at Jesus.

"Do you see those demons of lust out there?" Satan almost whispered. "Since I made them leave the orgies in Rome and come here they are nearly starving. Many of the people here have learned to feed on the Word of God. Many of the rest have learned to keep their passions in check with all of their traditions. But those lust demons are not as stupid as they appear. They can unravel those traditions, and even use them to sow more lust in the hearts of this weak people You and Your Father care so much about. After they give in to their lusts, these people become even more devoted to appearing pious on the outside in order to cover up the corruption in their hearts. The demons like that even more because it hides them better. As long as they can cause the lust to grow in the hearts of these people, their appetite is satisfied."

Lucifer watched the grief rise in Jesus' eyes. The Son of God mourned deeply as He thought of the spiritual and moral corruption of His own Father's bride, and His mother, the nation of Israel. The devil then continued,

> "You have probably witnessed how the lust that is now in some of the most pious men here, at least in their appearance, is even greater than we have ever seen in Rome. Of course, the demons of deception and the religious demons love this! Most of them have decided that they really do not want to return to Rome now since they have it so good here. I think that it will only be a short time before they have seduced even those who really love the Word of God."

Lucifer again looked at Jesus, who was grieved to the point of tears, which were now streaming down His face. The devil patiently let it all sink in, and then continued.

> "It seems that very soon this whole nation will be bowing down to me, just like the Romans and the Greeks before them. Of course, I will not bring the idols back. I must confess that what You did through the Maccabees has made that difficult here, but I don't really need idols with this religious façade. Having them reject idols caused those religious demons to show some creativity. Now they have learned how to get men to even make an idol out of the Scriptures, their traditions, and of course, their

own high religious titles and positions. The High Priest is now far more adored here than Your Father. Now they even esteem and trust the Pharisees more than Him, and the Pharisees love their leaders more than Him."

Lucifer again turned to look at Jesus, who remained silent but was grieving more and more.

"I really don't care to do this to this pitiful little people. It actually saddens me that Your Father really has no one on earth that loves Him, and I personally enjoy it much more in Rome now. But with all that You have planned through this people, we now have to concentrate our efforts on this little nation. If You are going to try to lead them back to obedience, to try to restore the rest of the world back to obedience, I must do all that I can to stop You. We are having so much success now that it will only be a matter of time before we have completely destroyed these people. That would be a pity. I really do not get any pleasure out of that. I do not know why You care so much for them, or why You care so much for men at all, but we do enjoy them for entertainment, and they are the only food we have now. And look how they actually enjoy the company of my demons more than they want to be with You or Your Father. They are very soon about to destroy themselves with their self-centeredness, and neither of us wants that, so I have thought of a solution that may work for both of us."

Lucifer again turned and looked at Jesus with what seemed to be the most genuine compassion. Pausing for just a few seconds, he continued in a slightly lower voice.

"I know You love these people. I know You want to help them. Neither do I care to go on destroying them like this. In fact, I, too, would rather be rid of these lowly demons and their sick perversions. This world is now mine. Adam gave it to me when he chose to serve me. At first I was just angry at God for banishing me from heaven. That is why I released all of these hordes with their perversions and diseases, but now I just want to exist in peace. If You will just acknowledge me as the lord here, I will let You rule over not only this little nation, but over all of the kingdoms of this world, as my main lieutenant. Then You can have them all living under that Law that You gave to Moses. You can make them righteous, and give them peace and joy. You would make a wonderful ruler in this realm! Do it for them."

Then Lucifer pointed at the evil horde that was darkening the sky.

"Then You can send all of these hordes to the pit, and I, too, will be glad to see them go. Then there will be no more wars or diseases, and men will begin to live as long as Adam again, a thousand years, or even longer if You will lift that ban and let them find the Tree of Life again. Then there will be peace on earth. I will let You do whatever You want. All You have to do is take one bow before me to acknowledge my legal right here, so that I know that the Father will not banish me from here as He did from heaven."

Jesus was looking intently at Lucifer. "I have Him right on the brink," the devil thought to himself. He waited to be sure that his next statement would hit with its maximum impact, pushing Him over the edge into the trap.

As Lucifer watched, the compassion he saw in Jesus for those poor people was even greater than he had thought. "How weak that compassion is making him," the devil pondered. "I must resolve to never let it get even the smallest grip on me. It is an enemy of true power."

Even so, the devil was the greatest of all masters at feigning compassion. It seemed to be working on Jesus like his other schemes had not. "False compassion is as strong as vengeance, if used properly," he thought, straining to hide the contempt he badly wanted to show for the Son, who had allowed Himself to fall to such a state of weakness in that frail human body. Gathering himself, Lucifer then offered what he knew would be the clincher.

"I know Your body is hurting You now. I do not know how You have endured being in it for so long. And to think that the Father wants You to endure several more years of it! But what I really do not understand is, if He really loved You, how could He possibly ask You, the Son of God, the Lord of glory, to endure the shame and torture He has planned for You? What could possibly be the reason for that? And for these pitiful little creatures? How could that possibly help them?"

After letting that sink in, he continued, "It was reasoning like that which caused me to turn against Him when I did. I remember Your glory. I cannot even bear to see You like this, much less on a Roman cross! Isn't that the 'tree' the Scriptures say that You are to be lifted up on? How could a loving Father do something like that to His Son? Just take one little bow to me and You can avoid all of that and return to Your glorious state imme-diately. It will be so easy, and so quick. Just do it, and then we can return this universe to some sanity."

After a pause Lucifer put on his best face of compassion. "Please. Let's just do it and get it over with," he entreated.

Then he waited again, sure that Jesus would bow at any moment. He studied Jesus' face, looking for any sign of His submission, but became concerned when the compassion on His face did not change. Finally Jesus turned and looked resolutely into the face of Lucifer.

"Depart from Me, Satan! The Scriptures say that 'You shall do homage to the Lord God, and Him alone shall you worship'" (see Matthew 4:10).

The smug arrogance turned quickly to terror, then rage, as Satan almost fell backward. He then retreated in haste. He knew that the Son had the power to destroy him with a word, or even a gesture. The fear that overwhelmed him quickly spread throughout the demonic hordes. They fled in every direction, as their terrified curses filled the air. Every angel in the region saw what was happening, and the praises of God and His Son quickly rose above the tumult of the fleeing demons. The Son had dispelled the evil one and his horde!

Michael and the captains who had been standing with him in their long and trying vigil now rushed to the Son.

"Lord, we thank the Father that You are okay! You endured the most terrible of all trials, and You have prevailed," Michael said as soon as they reached Him.

Jesus looked at the great archangel. "There will yet be a greater trial, but thank you for your encouragement."

"It was a terrible trial for us as well, watching You endure that onslaught of evil. We could not even see through the demonic cloud what was happening, but we could feel it. This whole part of the world could feel it. But thank the Father that You are alright! He told us to give You this bread, and to tell You how pleased He is in You."

At those words the eyes of Jesus glistened, and He stood to His feet with a strength that He had not felt for many days. Lifting His hands to heaven He cried out in great joy,

"Father, I am well pleased with You. All of Your ways are perfect. Thank You for My strength. Thank You for Your Spirit. Thank You for this bread, but even more, thank You for Your love and grace."

With that, Jesus sat back down on a rock and began to eat His bread.

"My friends," He said, looking up at Michael and the captains, "such bread is a simple but great pleasure that I have come to greatly appreciate as a man, but never as much as I do this loaf today. And after forty days of praying and fasting, seeing nothing but that evil cloud, I am just as thankful to see your faces as I am for this bread."

"Lord, we are honored to be with You now to comfort You. This time has been most difficult for all of us as well. We were all subject to Lucifer's guile when he tried to persuade us to rebel with him in heaven. We were in heaven, beholding the glory and majesty of the Father all around us, and it was still convincing, as many of our fellows gave in to it. Adam and Eve succumbed to it even while they were dwelling in Paradise with the Father's goodness all around them. It will forever be a marvel that You resisted his guile in such a weakened state, in the midst of such a wicked and evil world, even under such a cloud of depression! If any ever doubted that You were worthy of Your position, I do not think that they do now. We all now understand why You are the greatest joy of the Father."

As Michael looked at the Son, he marveled at Him even more than he did when He had agreed to become a Man and dwell on the earth among them. To all angels this had been incomprehensible, but for Him to endure the kind of temptation He had just suffered, this would cause all of the angels to marvel for the ages. The Son of God had certainly prevailed and proven that truth is stronger than the lie.

"Forgive me," Michael continued, "but You look very bad right now in Your body, even if in Your heart there is none like You. This is truly a day of glory and victory that we will forever rejoice in. You have defeated the devil—even in the form of a Man! The joy of Your Father and the joy in heaven has not been this great since we all sang together and the world came into being."

As Jesus stood, for a thousand miles in every direction the sky glistened with the swords of the angelic hosts that were drawn in a salute to Him. In heaven, the glory of the celebration was greater than had ever been witnessed before. Every angel, every cherubim, every created being in heaven, sang, danced, and rejoiced with all that was within them. Truth was victorious! New colors were born as the Father's delight overflowed to embrace the great hosts of angels and beings that He loved so much, which He and His Son had brought forth together.

Soon man, who had fallen to the depths of depravity and darkness, would be assured of one day beholding this glory, too. They were even now assured of one day beholding the greatest glory of all because they would rise from the greatest darkness of all. This was the greatest delight of the Father, to share beauty and glory with those who could see it and appreciate it. Beauty and glory were the result of His love, and He longed for those with whom He could share His love.

As Jesus began to walk along the dusty road from the wilderness, He could now feel the delight of the Father. All of the angels who lined the road, with their swords drawn in salute as they bowed on one knee, could also feel the Father's delight. This was the food of angels. Hours before it had been the darkest of times, and now it was the brightest. How quickly it had all changed!

The entire host that was with Michael and his commanders knew that the heavens were filled with the highest worship, but not one would now trade his place on the earth for what was happening in heaven. There would never again be a doubt that the King, even in His greatest weakness, was still much stronger than the evil one in his greatest strength.

Simon and Andrew were weary. They had fished all night without even catching enough for their breakfast. Andrew was just as weary of hearing Simon complain and chide him about his belief that Jesus was the Messiah. Andrew had to admit though that he, too, had even begun to have doubts. It seemed that Jesus would not be returning for them as He had promised.

It had now been many weeks, and not only had Jesus not returned, there had been no news of Him. After the great expectations that had arisen because of the Baptist, there now seemed to be a great pall of depression over the whole land. Not only had the skies been darkened by clouds for days, but great storms had whipped the land like a scourge. It was almost as if Jehovah had forsaken them altogether and was venting His wrath on them. Andrew now felt that the darkness in his heart was as great as the darkness over the land. It did seem as if Jesus had just disappeared.

The argument between the two brothers over the work that needed to be done to secure the boat was rising to a crescendo. Then they heard a great commotion coming from the town. They both stopped to look as it got louder, and was obviously coming toward them. It sounded like a wedding celebration, but it was much too early for that. As a young boy came around the corner, they called to him, "What is this about, young man?"

"A great Prophet has come to us! The One who heals the sick!"

Simon and Andrew looked at each other. Finally Simon asked, "What does he mean by 'The One who heals the sick'?"

"I do not know. I guess we have been out so long that we have missed the news that the others have heard. But at least He has come! This must be Jesus."

At that time the whole crowd came around the corner, with Jesus walking in the front. Without hesitation He came right up to Andrew and Simon, stepped down into their boat, and asked them to cast off. Simon hesitated, scowled, and then pushed off.

They had not gone far when Jesus raised His hand for them to stop. He then began to speak to the crowd, which had by now spread out all along the docks and seemed to fill every available place. Simon marveled, but had resolved not to be taken in like the rest by another prophet who promised deliverance, but could not deliver.

As Jesus taught the people, Andrew and Simon sat in the back of the boat and watched. Even Simon had to admire the way His words flowed over the great crowd like a gentle breeze. It settled them and gave them hope. He talked about God as if He were the people's close friend. He made God personal. He made them feel like God was right there with them.

After about an hour, Jesus told the people to go to their homes to enjoy each other and rest. They did not want to go, but they began to depart. There was such rejoicing that Simon wondered if he had ever seen a group of people so happy. A half dozen songs broke out from different groups as they walked along, and from the boat they seemed to form a harmony.

Simon and Andrew both sat speechless as the Lord turned to them, "Put out into the deep water and let down your nets."

After a moment Simon replied, "Sir, we have fished all night and caught nothing." Jesus said nothing. Finally, after a few minutes, Simon offered, "At Your bidding we will try again."

"Right here will be fine," Jesus said after they had paddled out a bit.

Andrew and Simon let the nets down. Simon was disgusted because he knew there had never been fish caught in this spot. However, as soon as their nets hit the water they were filled with more fish than they had ever caught before. Soon the nets even began to break. Seeing their neighbors nearby, Simon waved to them to come help. Jesus just sat looking on as they filled both boats with such a great quantity of fish that they were about to sink.

When they had finished, Simon and Andrew sat down and looked at Jesus. Simon remembered what he had said to Andrew when he told him how he believed that Jesus was the Messiah. Simon had ridiculed him, saying that he was glad that the Messiah was coming back for him, and that maybe He could tell them where the fish were. Simon knew somehow that Jesus knew of this statement. Certainly, this was a great Prophet!

Andrew was thinking about the same conversation, and about how he had replied that this was expecting too much of the Messiah, that only God could do that. He thought about what the Baptist had said of Him, how even the Baptist was not worthy to untie His sandals.

Both Andrew and Simon looked down at all of the fish, then at each other. They looked over at the other boats that were also struggling to haul in the great load of fish. They then looked up at Jesus. He was looking at them. A great fear gripped Simon as he fell to his knees.

"Please Master! Depart from me. I am a sinful man. I am not worthy for You to be in my boat!"

"I am not here because you are worthy," Jesus replied. "But I am here for Andrew and for you. Will you come?"

Simon began to weep uncontrollably. Andrew put his arms around him, and turned to Jesus.

"We cannot understand why You would want us, but we will both come."

Zebedee was becoming increasingly concerned over his son John. He now seemed despondent that Jesus had not returned for him as He had promised. James, John's brother, felt otherwise. He thought that John was overly idealistic and that this disappointment would be good for him.

But Zebedee did not like watching his son go from being so depressed that he could hardly work, to working with such frustration that it seemed as if every task was an enemy that needed to be punished. Zebedee decided that it had gone too far and he had to talk to him.

"My son, I know that you put much trust in this Jesus, but we should not put such trust in any man. Only God is worthy of such trust.

He alone will never disappoint us. He is the only One we should devote ourselves to in such a way. Even the greatest prophets like Moses and Elijah made mistakes. It is because we as a people have been so easily prone to follow after men that we are now suffering this terrible yoke of being under the Romans. We have only received what we deserved for not determining to have no other King but Jehovah."

John did not even look up to acknowledge his father's words. They each hit him like a slap in the face, even though he believed that what he was saying was true. True or not, he did not want to hear or believe them. He just did not know what to do. The months that he had spent with John the Baptist had been the most wonderful of his life. They had been filled with continual wonder at the Lord's activity. The Baptist stirred hopes of a greater move of God than Israel had ever experienced. Never had he felt such hope, such expectation, and such wonder. Now the disappointment seemed to be just as terrible as those times had been wonderful. Even so, this time at home had confirmed to him that he could never go back to a normal life again, but he just did not know what he could do. Would the Baptist take him back as a disciple?

John looked up at his father, whom he loved and respected greatly. "Father, I agree with what you are saying. I know that I will some-how get beyond the disorientation I now feel. But I know that I must either return to the Baptist or somehow find Jesus. I cannot blame Jesus for not keeping His word. Anyone can forget. Something may have come up that prevented Him from coming.

"I will go find Him!" John blurted out, throwing down the net he had been mending. This resolve was like a wind blowing away the fog from his mind. Suddenly, he felt better. "I will seek Jesus until I find Him! If I have to I will not even eat until I do, but I will find Him," he continued with such force that it shocked his father and brother.

"Whenever you seek Me you will find Me," a voice flowed down from the bank above them. All three of the men wheeled around to see who had spoken.

"Master!" John shouted, leaping up the bank in giant strides. "You came for me!"

"Did you doubt that I would?"

"Well, it has been so long," John mumbled.

"Did you doubt My word?" Jesus asked again.

John did not know what to say, so he did not say anything. Jesus did not say anything either, but continued to look straight at him. Finally, John almost whispered, "I'm sorry. I did begin to doubt . . . but I knew that You must have had a good reason not to have come."

"I understand, but you will learn that you never have reason to doubt My word," Jesus replied, as He reached out to take John's hand and pull him to the top of the bank.

Jesus then turned and looked down upon Zebedee and James. Both had been watching the scene with great interest. John quickly spoke up, "Father, brother, forgive me for not introducing you. This is Jesus, whom I told you about."

"Yes," Zebedee replied, "our son has told us much about You. Can we please offer You hospitality in our home?"

"Sir, My Father and I have always appreciated the hospitality We have received in your home, as well as in the home of your father. That is why I have come for your sons, so that they can help to build Us a house. Then I will receive you and your father and show you hospitality."

Zebedee obviously did not understand Him. "Sir, have You been here before?" he asked.

"Friend, it is hard for you to understand now, but you will later. You and your house have honored God by seeking to know His ways, and by teaching your sons to trust Him. He will now honor you by using your sons."

As He was talking, He reached out His hand to pull James to the top of the bank. James took His hand shyly. "Will you join us?" Jesus asked, gazing intently at James.

James was stunned. A flood of thoughts arose from his heart. He had never considered himself a spiritual person like his brother. He tried to live by the rules and sincerely tried to do what was right, mostly to honor his father and mother, but he had really never felt much of a desire to know about God. God seemed too ambiguous and hard to understand. He had felt a subtle and almost continuous guilt about this, but now it was more than that. For some reason, at this moment, he felt shame that he had not wanted to know more about God. The presence of Jesus magnified these feelings in him to the point that he felt that he would either have to run or weep.

"Do not be ashamed. You are no different from other men. No man desires to know God. Many do want to honor Him, but few want to know Him, and even fewer want to be close to Him. But the Father wants to be close to men, and He wants to be close to you. He wants to use you to help bring men closer to Him."

Each word seemed to hit James like a hammer upon his breast. John and his father were even embarrassed as tears began to flow down James' face. They had never seen him this emotional before, and he had never felt that way before. He was truly sorry that he had not tried to know God. He was also happier than he could ever remember being as he considered what Jesus had just said to him. He could not only get close to God, but he was sure that somehow the Lord was asking him to right now!

"Master, please just tell me what I need to do."

"Follow Me."

"I do not know You, but I somehow know that You are true. I feel as if God Himself is speaking through You. You not only know what I am thinking, You are somehow drawing my deepest thoughts out of my heart. I have never felt like this, and I do not do things rashly, but I know that I will follow You. I will."

Zebedee watched the entire scene in stunned silence. How could such a brief encounter with a stranger have such an impact on his son? And why was it that in spite of his astonishment, he was not feeling dismay, but peace? He felt that, even as crazy as it all seemed, it was right. In fact, he even felt excitement.

Jesus then turned and looked at Zebedee. As He did, Zebedee felt something that he had not felt since he was a young child. He called it the "joyful presence." When he sat on the edge of the sea pondering the glory of all that God had made, he would begin to feel as if the Lord Himself would join him. Many times he had asked the Lord to show him His glory just as He had shown it to Moses. He was always afraid that the Lord would do it, but he had determined that, as frightening as it might be, it would be worth it. The feeling of the joyful presence that would often come upon him at such times was the greatest feeling he had ever had. He knew that if he were able to ever visibly see the Lord's glory, it would be an ecstasy beyond anything that he could ever otherwise experience. As he had grown and taken on many responsibilities, he had not returned to such times of reflection and the joy he used to have in just pondering the Lord. Now, so abruptly, that same joy was all over him. He felt that joyful presence. This changed everything for him. Immediately, he understood John and hoped that James would experience this.

"Master," Zebedee almost whispered. "I used to pray to see the glory of the Lord. I never did, but I know that I have felt His nearness. I feel Him now. Maybe it is not for me to see His glory, but if my sons go with You, I know that they, too, will know the joy of His presence. This would be my greatest joy for me now, for my sons to go with You. I know in my heart that You have been sent by God to visit our land. Our land needs His presence more than anything.

"Our family prayer, which I have heard all of my life, and which my sons have heard all of their lives, is that our family would be used to bring honor to the great name of our God. Somehow, I know that You are here because of those prayers. I will miss my sons, but this is a great day for me. I thank the God of my fathers for hearing our prayers."

"Friend, your prayers have been heard, and you will see the glory of God. God also knows what it means to send His Son. You have given Him two, and He will reward you. He will reward you with the closeness to Him that you have desired all of your life.

"I will come to you again and enjoy the hospitality that you have offered, but now we must depart. I have a purpose for which I cannot delay, and you have an old Friend who has missed the times that you used to have together."

Zebedee arose, climbed the small bank, and embraced each of his sons. As he turned to face Jesus, he felt the great Presence with even more intensity. His brow furrowed as he tried to hold back the flood of tears that were about to erupt. Jesus reached out and touched his shoulder, and then turned and departed with James and John close behind Him.

Zebedee watched them turn the corner. He felt sadness at the departure of his sons, but he also felt a great joy. He stepped back into the boat and just sat for awhile. Then he pushed off. He was going to spend the night on the water. He had a Friend whom he had not been with for a very long time, and he could not do anything else until he got alone with Him again.

"I'm sorry that I ever grew up and lost what I had with You then," Zebedee prayed. "I must become a child again. I must never again lose what I had then, and what I felt when Jesus came here today. I may have lost my sons today, but it will be worth it if I regain my closeness to You. That alone could help me endure this loss."

Simon and Andrew watched the encounter with Zebedee and his sons with great interest. Andrew was glad to see his friend John, but Simon had already started to feel a little possessive of Jesus. Even so, Simon was astonished by the whole encounter with Zebedee and his sons. He had to fight his own emotions as hard as he could to keep from crying with them. He had never seen Zebedee like this before, but he began to feel a love for him as if he were his own father. He was even now sorry that they had to leave him so quickly.

For almost an hour the men walked on in a slightly awkward silence. Finally, Simon spoke up.

"Master, where are we going?"

"We are going to the house of Israel," Jesus replied. "We will start in Galilee, and then we will move from place to place as the Father leads us. We must go to the whole house of Israel."

"But what will we be doing?" Andrew ventured.

"We will be doing more than you can now understand, even if I were to explain it to you. Even so, please ask Me what is on your heart to know. I want you to understand everything, but some things you just will not understand until you have experienced them."

This encouraged Simon and the others. Soon they were all trying to ask Him questions at once. Jesus stopped, raised His hand for silence, and then began to explain to them something that they had not asked, but which somehow appeased all of their other questions.

"My ultimate desire for you is that you understand as I do, and that you will do the works that I do. Therefore, I will *do* and then *teach*. You must not be satisfied to just see My works, but you are called to understand them and then to do them yourselves. For this reason, I will always welcome your questions. After you grow in faith to do My works, you must teach others to do the same."

"Master, what works are You talking about? Are we going to be baptizing, like John? Or will You do something else?" John asked.

"Yes, we will at times baptize, but I am talking about other works. Tomorrow you will begin to see them and understand."

Just hearing conversation after the group had walked so far in the awkward silence was a relief. Quickly, there was almost a buoyancy in the group. The uncomfortable feelings were displaced by a deep, but sober joy. As the joy permeated the group, Simon's protectiveness toward Jesus was displaced by thankfulness that others had also joined them. He walked over to talk to the sons of Zebedee. After a while longer, Jesus called for James to walk beside Him so that they could talk.

"The shame that you felt earlier, when you first saw Me, was the same guilt that Adam felt, which caused him to hide from God after his sin. All men are still hiding from

Him. This shame has all men in bondage and alienated from God. Because of this, they do not want to see God or hear Him but He created man to be close to Him. My Father longs to be close to men, and though they resist it, all men truly long in their deepest hearts to be close to Him. That is why I am here, and that is why you are with Me—to help reconcile men with their God."

James did not reply, but he immediately understood what Jesus was talking about. After a few moments, He continued:

"There are many ways in which men hide from God because of their shame. Many in Israel even hide from Him by zealously trying to serve Him, performing sacrifices and devoting themselves to religious activity. But they do not worship Him with this activity; they are worshiping their own works. They are, by this, putting their trust in their own works more than in Him. All who truly desire to serve God must do what you did. They must choose not to hide, but to come out into the light of My Father's presence. You are called to be one of My evangelists, and that is your job—to help men come out of their hiding places to stand in the presence of God."

"Sir, turning to You instead of away from You was one of the hardest things I have ever done. I really do not even know how I was able to do it."

"You received help," Jesus replied. "No man can come to Me unless the Father helps them. No amount of human persuasion can release a man from the great bondage that shame has on his heart. That is why you must come to know the Holy Spirit, whom My Father will send to testify of Me to all He is calling back to Himself. It was not just My words that persuaded you, but a knowledge that came to your heart that I was true. It is the Holy Spirit who makes My words living and like sharp swords, able to cut the yokes that are upon the hearts of men. As My evangelist, you will be entrusted with the same power in your words, which will testify of Me."

"Sir," James responded. "If I had not had the experience, I know that I could not understand what You are talking about. Because of what I just experienced, I do understand. But I have never thought of anything like this before."

"And neither has anyone else. This is why I must *do* and then *teach*. I have not come to work in the same way that any man has worked before. My works are from above, and men who are from the earth cannot understand them until they have been helped by the Holy Spirit. The ways of God are different than the ways of men. He does not think like men, but religious men believe that He thinks just like they do. Therefore, religious men are the most difficult men for the Holy Spirit to help. It was much easier for you to understand and come to Me because you were not a religious man."

James was really surprised by this statement. "I always thought that religious men were the closest to God."

"No. Really you did not think that. Deep in your heart you knew that was not the way to God. Deep in your heart you knew that the Lord was not concerned about rituals and sacrifices. In your heart, you felt that God must be above all of that, and you were right."

"Then why are so many of our holy men so zealous for these rituals?" James asked, still troubled by the thought that these men were not serving God, though they were devoting their lives to this service.

"One act of kindness means more to God than a lifetime of performing rituals. Rituals can have their place if they are used to stir men to love, but they are enemies of truth when they are used to take the place of love," Jesus replied, turning and saying it loudly enough for the rest to hear.

"Rituals can be one of the thickest cloaks that men will use to try to hide from God. I have come to strip away this cloak so that men can come out of hiding, walk in truth, and walk with the Lord again just as Adam did before the Fall.

"You are now with Me because you made the decision not to hide from God or yourself. You did this because the Holy Spirit gave you peace in your hearts and the knowledge that I am true. The Holy Spirit is a Helper—He does not force Himself upon men. Only when a man chooses to come out of hiding into His light can He help them. He moves upon them to draw them to the Father, but He does not push, and you must not try to force men either. That is not Our way, and that is not the way to life."

Jesus, who had been walking ahead with James, then stopped and faced His new disciples and continued, "Religious men are the most resistant to the help of the Holy Spirit. This is because they have built their lives on trust in their own righteousness, which they use to cover up their shame for the unrighteousness they feel in their hearts. For a man to get free, he must allow the shame to be exposed, acknowledge it, and be willing to come into the light in order to be set free. Shame is self-centeredness in place of God-centeredness. It is for this reason that the publicans and harlots will come to God before those who consider themselves righteous."

James was even more surprised by this statement. "Do you mean that publicans and harlots can come to God?"

"Yes," Jesus replied. "They are all loved by the Father. He loves all men, even the self-righteous, though they are much harder for Him to reach."

"Please forgive me if I am presumptuous, but You almost make it sound as if the publicans and sinners are closer to God and that the religious ones are the furthest from Him. I understand what You are saying about how rituals are misused, but it is hard to believe that those who give themselves to lives of sin can more easily come to God," James almost whispered, as if he did not want anyone else to hear him.

"It is a hard saying, but it is true," Jesus replied. "Many of the worst sinners will come

to Me before those who appear to be the most religious and upstanding citizens. Pride caused the devil to fall, and has caused the fall of almost everyone since. Pride is to think that you do not need God. Pride is to think that you could ever be righteous or acceptable on your own merit.

"Self-righteousness is what caused Satan to fall from grace. He is actually one of the most religious beings in the creation. That is why he usually appears as if he were an angel of light. Those who follow him the closest try to appear the same and are usually deceived into thinking that they have more light than anyone else. Only the humble will acknowledge their shame instead of trying to cover it up. Only the humble will acknowledge that they are in the darkness and need the light. That is why Isaiah said:

Who is blind but My servant, or so deaf as My messenger whom I send? Who is so blind as he that is at peace with Me, or so blind as the servant of the Lord?

You have seen many things, but you do not observe them; your ears are open, but none hears.

The Lord was pleased for His righteousness' sake to make the law great and glorious.

> But this is a people plundered and despoiled; all of them are trapped in caves, or are hidden away in prisons; they have become a prey with none to deliver them, and a spoil, with none to say, "Give them back!"
>
> Who among you will give ear to this? Who will give heed and listen hereafter? (Isaiah 42:19-23)

This passage, which had been considered an incomprehensible enigma to most scholars, was now easily understood by the disciples. It even seemed obvious to them, and their exhilaration from this revelation was great. No teacher had been able to make the Scriptures come alive like this!

Jesus continued, "Satan fell because he allowed pride to enter his heart. Therefore, God will only give His grace to the humble. The Law was great and glorious, but it could only help those who would humble themselves before it. When men see the Law, and exalt themselves with it, using it to declare themselves righteous and able to keep it, this is the greatest form of pride, and they will use it for an even greater evil. They will use it to plunder their brothers with it, just as was spoken through Isaiah. But the humble face the Law that reveals the righteousness of God and acknowledge that it is beyond them. These are the ones who will come to God, those who know they need His help and His redemption."

The group walked along for a few minutes. James was in deep thought, as this was so new to him. He had respected the most those whom Jesus said were probably the furthest from God. He had respected the least those whom He said were the closest. As if knowing His thoughts, Jesus looked straight at James as He continued.

"It is not right to think that the ways of the publicans and sinners are closest to God. They are not close to Him either when they are in their sin. However, they will more easily come to Him because they know that they are in darkness, and they will more quickly humble themselves to acknowledge their need for help. The self-righteous will be offended by even the suggestion that they need help. Because God has given man the freedom to choose, man must choose to accept His help. He will only do this to the degree that he knows how badly he needs help.

"When Lucifer began to think that the light and power that he had came from himself, he turned from God to serve himself. Men who follow in his ways feel the same. This was the first transgression—the first turning away from God. It is the most difficult to free men of. To help men, the Holy Spirit will reveal to them their shame, illuminating their sin. It is at that point that they must choose to either receive His help, as you did, or go even deeper into hiding from His presence. Those who go deeper into hiding, whether it is by covering themselves with sin or with the Law, will fight the light with a greater ferocity, thinking that the light that threatens them is actually darkness. If they would listen to their hearts, they would know that this is not true, but those who go this way ceased listening to their hearts long ago.

"Earlier, you understood your sin, how you had tried to live by the rules, and how you did not do this for God, but for yourself. You confronted this and decided to repent, to turn to Me and follow Me. This was the most important choice that you have ever made or ever will make. Even so, there are other areas of your lives that are still hidden from God, which will be exposed as we walk together, and you will have to make the same choice each time.

"When you see darkness in your own heart, do not try to hide it. If you will not hide, you will always be set free. Your lives will be filled with both more freedom and more joy.

Do not run from Me, but to Me. I will never be surprised or shocked by what is in your heart, because I have already seen it. I will never condemn you; I have come to set you free.

"When you are free, you must set others free with the same freedom that you have received. Never take pride in your freedom or look down upon those who are not yet free, even the self-righteous. The Father loves all men, even those who resist Him. Your main job from this day on is to love. You must love God above all, and love men even as you learn to love yourself again. To love yourself as you should is not self-centeredness, but the joy of being a child of God."

The disciples were all feeling this joy now. They also understood how, at the same time, they felt terribly unworthy to be walking with Him and to be taught by Him personally. At times, they wanted to run, and at times they knew they would endure the revealing of any sin or shame in order to stay close to Him. This was a feeling they would have to get used to as layer after layer of the hardness of their hearts was stripped away.

After a time, Jesus continued again. "What I am saying to you now will become increasingly more clear as we walk together. This is the foundation of My purpose and your purpose. Always keep in mind that when My Father saw the sin of this world, He did not condemn it; it was already condemned. He sent Me to save the world. I am here to proclaim liberty to the captives, and to be a light to those who have hidden in darkness. I will receive any who will come out of the darkness into My light.

"It always hurts to have the darkness that you have been hiding in stripped away by the light. Even so, it is the path of freedom, and after you have been delivered the pain will have been worth it. You are with Me to help men come out of hiding, to remove that with which they have tried to cover themselves, so that they can stand before Me with nothing between us. Then I will cover their nakedness with light.

"When you feel exposed, do not hide, but come to Me. The more that you learn you can trust Me, the more you will be willing to be exposed to My light. Trust cannot be forced. We must therefore allow men to walk by faith, not by force. True faith begins by coming out of hiding to be exposed to the light. True faith is to be willing to be naked, exposed, and vulnerable, knowing that I have not come to hurt you, but to help you. Faith in My intentions, and My power to help, is the most powerful force in the creation. You will learn this. It is more powerful than the pride of men or devils, and it will crush their strongholds over men.

"You and this little group are the beginning of a great march of truth. It will be a long march, but men will come to believe Me. As they do, and they come out of hiding, the power of the light will grow in them. The release of this power will enable many others to know that they, too, can trust Me and come out of hiding. This power will grow in those who come to Me, until one day they are used to do greater exploits than have ever been done on this earth."

"Master, do You mean greater miracles?" blurted out Simon, who had been trying to catch every word of the conversation between James and Jesus.

"Yes, I mean greater miracles. The greatest miracles that God has done upon the earth have not even required the lifting of His little finger. Just as He has parted seas, He will one day part mountains, because of the prayers of faith that come from little children who trust Him."

Michael and the captains who stood with him were also listening to all that Jesus had said, as were the thousands of angels who stood all around them. As a peaceful silence had come upon the little group that walked along the dusty road with Jesus, one of the captains spoke up.

"I have been here since the devil was allowed to tempt the first man and woman, but I have never understood the great evil that lies in men or the fallen angels like I do now. What Satan tried to tell us was that this weakness is really the source of our strength. He tried to cause us to rebel by enticing us to come to know ourselves and live by what he calls 'the great light that is within each of us.' I have often been concerned that I never felt that there was a great light within me, but that I only had what the Father had given me. I have not understood why it seemed that the more I felt this way—that I was lacking in great light and power within me, the more I felt dependent on the Father, the higher I was promoted. Now I see that this is the truth that upholds the creation—we only have what we have been given. The more we know that all power and light come from the Father, the more we can be trusted with power and authority."

"That is why men will one day even judge us," Michael offered. "Those who have fallen into such depravity and darkness, who are so weak and blind, will know even more deeply their dependence on the Father. Therefore, He will trust them with more authority, because they will know that they cannot trust in themselves, but are dependent on Him. Such will not again make the mistake that Satan made.

"That is why the Son has become one of them—to help them to come out of hiding and into the light of God once again. Now we are learning more about God every day than we have learned since the beginning. How great is the blessing that we have received, to be here and able to see these things!

"How blessed are these men who come to Him, who hear His words and behold the glory of His ways. To behold this has truly been worth all of the battles. All of the darkness that our enemy has brought into the creation only makes the glory of our God much brighter. The Father is more worthy of our allegiance than I have ever considered before. He truly is the Source of all authority, power, glory, and dominion! How great and wonderful are these times," Michael continued.

The mood among the little band of disciples who walked with Jesus was becoming more sober. It had begun to sink in just how profound the difference was between what Jesus had just shared with them about a true relationship to God, and their whole religious foundation, which indeed the entire nation was now founded upon. They could all see how profoundly the nation was about to be rocked with Jesus' message.

John and Andrew both began to understand just how the Baptist's message really did prepare the way for Jesus. Their hearts had been prepared for Him by the long time that they had been with the Baptist, but they knew that most of the nation, especially its leaders, were going to have a very hard time with Him. Both still could not understand how it could be that their religion had come to be so directly opposed to the very One they presumed to be worshiping.

Jesus, knowing their thoughts and letting them run their course for a time, then stopped again and faced them, saying,

> "You each had your own conflict to overcome to be here. You each had to choose Me over that which you had veiled your own heart with. Everyone will have this same conflict, and so will the nation. The veil is thick and ancient. No one can come to Me without surrendering what they have made to try to cover their own sins, just as Adam did in the

Garden. All men try to hide from God just as he did. I am the Father's love to provide men with a covering for their sins and to beckon them to come out of hiding and draw close to Him again.

"The battle for the heart of this nation began with the Baptist, but now we must continue it. Many will be set free, but those who will not come to the light will hate light, and they will hate Me and hate you. For this reason, you will know conflict every day that you walk with Me. In this world you will have conflict, trouble, and continuous opposition, but I will give you a peace that will overcome the world so that you will even have joy in the midst of your persecutions. This peace can only come from knowing that you are doing the will of My Father. That peace must control you instead of the fear of man. If you live by the fear of man, you will not be able to help men. Fear God and Him only. That is the way of peace."

The disciples knew that this was an ultimate question. What would control them: the fear of man or the fear of God? The answer to this question would more than anything else determine if they could follow Him or not. For most in their nation, it would be whether they would give up their own righ-teousness which they had worked their whole lives to establish, working hard almost every day to maintain, and exchange it for faith in Jesus. To others, the ulti-mate question would be whether they loved their sin more than they would love Him. Some would soon be added to their group that had to answer this question. The mix of these personalities would blend together as they walked with Him together until they became the most powerful little band of people to ever walk the earth.